Divine Memories
of
Sathya Sai Baba

by

Diana Baskin

With love and Blessings! Sri Sath Sai

This book may be obtained at your local bookstore or you may order it directly from Birth Day Publishing Company, P. O. Box 7722, San Diego, California 92107.

Library of Congress Catalog Card Number 90-60347

ISBN 1-878599-00-3

Published by Birth Day Publishing Company
P. O. Box 7722, San Diego, California 92107, USA

Dedicated
at the Lotus Feet
of my beloved Lord
Bhagavan Sri Sathya Sai Baba

Sai Baba's Sarvadharma emblem represents the unity among the five major religions of the world.

Table of Contents

Bhagavan Sri Sathya Sai Baba born November 23, 1926.

DISSATISFACTION WITH THE WORLD

There are four things in which every man must interest himself: Who am I? Wherefrom have I come? Whither am I going? How long shall I be here? All spiritual inquiry begins with these questions and attempts to find out the answers.

Sathya Sai Baba

At twenty-four I was married to a man who loved excitement, parties and nightclubs. He was a former actor, director and writer. I was working as a social secretary for the Italian government, assisting in fashion shows and wine-tasting parties and promoting exports of Italian goods to the United States. Between the office and my husband, I was in the stream of social life in Los Angeles, constantly going to parties and exclusive Beverly Hills nightclubs.

Buried deep beneath this layer of worldliness, a nagging question persisted: What is the purpose of life? Each time the question arose, it would quickly be buried in the many worldly distractions, only to surface with more intensity the next time. Finally, I reached a point when all experiences which had previously given me happiness created within me only a feeling of emptiness and dissatisfaction.

In my youth, while accompanying my mother throughout the world in her search for truth, I had met many who claimed to be genuine teachers. Later, I found them to be no more than mere mortals, hiding their weaknesses publicly and not practicing what they preached privately. Perhaps, because of these early disappointments, I became very doubtful about the existence of God. I questioned whether any living being had been able to discover and achieve the purpose of life. Religion, which seemed to me to be based more upon faith and less upon reason, gave me few answers. I preferred Buddha's advice: Do not believe anything anybody tells you unless you have yourself experienced it. I was convinced that only by experience could I gain the necessary faith to understand and reach the goal of life.

My pressing question was soon answered in more ways than I ever expected when my mother returned from her first trip to India and told me, that not only had she found a guru but a sadguru, a teacher of teachers. She was not so presumptuous as to say He was an avatar, because it would take a person in that consciousness to recognize an incarnation of divinity, but that was His declaration and she believed it, so uniquely different was He from any being she had ever seen. Pure love, capable of uplifting and transforming, radiated from Him. His words were soft, consoling and awakening and revealed His total awareness of every aspect of our lives. Every thought, action and feeling we ever experienced were bare before Him.

He could instantly produce whatever object or food He willed by a wave of His hand. She showed me a pendant shaped like a fish, inset with rubies, pearls and diamonds which He had materialized for her and, for my stepfather a semiprecious stone and metal portrait of Himself.

He materialized vibhuti (sacred ash) for His devotees that had great spiritual and curative properties; it could cure any disease and even bring the dead back to life. Had anyone other than my mother told me these things I would not have believed them. It sounded incredible; I had to see this phenomenon called Sai Baba.

When Mother offered to accompany me to India, I announced my plans to my husband but he was not interested in the least in what I did or said about Sai Baba. While I had gradually stopped going to night clubs and parties and doing many of the things he was fond of, he remained totally involved, needing these activities as a drug to keep himself constantly stimulated. Our marriage was in serious trouble. Although I was pregnant with our first child, I was determined to go to India. My leaving, I am sure, was a relief for my husband as he could now forget our difficulties and return without interference to his all-consuming pleasures.

Author took this photo of Sai Baba in Brindavan.

THE JOURNEY

*Life is a pilgrimage where man drags his feet
along the rough and thorny road. With the
name of God on his lips, he will have no thirst;
with the form of God in his heart, he will feel
no exhaustion. The company of the holy will
inspire him to travel in hope and faith. The
assurance that God is within calling distance,
that He is ever near, and that He is not long
in coming will lend strength to his limb and
courage to his eye.*

Sathya Sai Baba

Deciding to take full advantage of our trip, we
bought a round-the-world ticket. We planned to stop in
several countries before and after our stay in India, as there
were no obligations to hurry or return at any specific time.
I did not understand then that I was setting out on a sacred
pilgrimage, one that should be undertaken only with a spirit
of reverence and a single-pointed goal, instead of combining
it with such frivolous distractions as sightseeing.

On our first stop in Hawaii, we had a grand time enjoying the beauty of nature in a convertible jeep which we rented and drove to every corner of that magnificent tropical island.

In Hong Kong, we took the ferry to the Chinese border and walked for miles through the hills and the busy city. We visited a Hindu temple where I met an old pundit (priest) who, when I told him we were on our way to see Sai Baba, folded his hands in reverence and said gravely: "Sai Baba is a very great being. It is such a privilege just to have His darshan (sight of a holy man). You will be most fortunate if He even talks to you." His words puzzled me as I never doubted that Sai Baba would see and talk to me. I was coming all the way from America just to see Him; why would He not see me?   Don't all holy men receive visitors that are serious seekers? I wondered. After all, my mother had been received immediately and had many private interviews, including two spiritual talks each day. I discounted the validity of the old pundit's words but throughout the trip I could never entirely forget what he had said. I had no idea whatsoever of Sai Baba's grandeur.

In Bangkok, the sidewalks were very uneven and full of potholes. While we were walking on the irregular pavement, my mother stumbled and broke her toe. She has never had much faith in doctors and always tried to avoid them. So, I knew better than to insist that Mother see a doctor and did precisely what she requested: I packed her foot in ice and for three days she lay in bed until the scheduled departure of the flight to Delhi. By the time of our departure, she was barely able to walk and was still limping badly. Our plane arrived in Delhi at two in the morning and we took a taxi to the hotel booked by our travel agent. When we entered the dimly lit lobby and saw ladies walking about half dressed in transparent skirts, we hurried from the shady place in search of another hotel.

All the hotels we went to were full. Finally, one took pity, and put us up in the servants' quarters on a cot that collapsed in the middle of the night injuring my mother. In the morning, out of desperation, we called a gentleman whose phone number had been given to us by a friend in case we needed a contact in Delhi. We hoped that he could find us a hotel room for a few days until we could catch our flight to Bangalore. The man we called was very kind and told us he would make all arrangements and come to pick us up right away.

When he came for us, we expected him to take us to another hotel and were dumbfounded when he told us he had called his guru's ashram (a religious community), and it was our good fortune to be accepted. He packed us on a train with instructions not to open the windows or talk to anyone during the six-hour ride. What could we say? He was so kind; we had no place to stay, no choice, so we went.

The ashram was beautiful. We were given a furnished, private room with beds, chairs, desk and western bath. There was a large cafeteria that served delicious vegetarian food and most of the visitors were Westerners. They would gather every evening with their guru, a well-known Sikh Master, for question-and-answer sessions. The guru has a large following throughout the world and disciples have been initiated for centuries by a long line of masters. One afternoon the guru called my mother and me for a private interview. I felt nothing extraordinary being with or talking to him, only the impression that he was kinder and wiser than most humans but still human.

I kept pressing my mother to leave because I was very anxious to see Sai Baba, but she needed very much to rest because her toe was causing considerable pain. A devotee doctor at the ashram had confirmed it was broken but she still would not allow any treatment. She urged me to enjoy the food and accommodations and to rest up before the unexpected. She never had the courage to tell me what Sai Baba's ashram was like, and I had no idea of the primitive conditions —and unexpected welcome— that were in store for me!

THE PUNDIT'S PROPHECY COMES TRUE

*Journey through life in courage, joy, peace,
charity and above all humility.*

Sathya Sai Baba

When we arrived in Bangalore, we went to the West End Hotel; it was a modern, first-class hotel. In the dining room we met an Indian couple, Mr. and Mrs. Ratanlal, devotees of Sai Baba. They told us Sai Baba would be inaugurating the opening of His women's college in Anantapur the next day and that the President of India was scheduled to give the inaugural speech. They planned to attend the ceremonies and invited us to join them in their taxi.

In the morning, my mother started feeling very sick but urged me to join the Ratanlals and go without her. There was a large crowd when we arrived and I was able to see Sai Baba only from a great distance. I sat very uncomfortably cross-legged on the ground among masses of people throughout long, tedious talks in Indian languages. While all the time I was burning with desire to meet Sai Baba and thinking that this was not at all what I had expected of our first meeting.

When the talks and celebrations were over, I followed the Ratanlals to the college courtyard area where only a few people were allowed to enter. There, a handful of devotees had gathered to wait for Sai Baba. Finally Sai Baba appeared! I held my breath and felt my heart pounding in anticipation of that great moment when He would greet me with a smile of recognition and say something like: "You have come, I have been waiting for you, my beloved disciple."

He walked directly towards me and was all smiles as He greeted Mrs. Ratanlal on my right and Mr. Ratanlal on my left; He ignored me completely. Sai Baba made me feel invisible, small and humiliated. While He was chatting with the Ratanlals, the old pundit's words flashed in my mind: they had come true. I felt such deep pain and rejection on the ride back to Bangalore that all my pent-up emotion turned to anger. I chain-smoked the entire four hours and practically asphyxiated the Ratanlals. By the time we reached the hotel my boiling anger had turned into a high temperature!

FIRST INTERVIEW

You may be seeing me today for the first time,
but you are all old acquaintances for Me. I
know you through and through.

Sathya Sai Baba

By morning, both Mother and I had high temperatures. The fever had burned away my anger and made me
too tired to think or analyze what had happened the previous day. Were it not for my mother's faith, I would have
been too discouraged to go on but she convinced me it
would be better for us to be ill in the atmosphere of the
ashram than in the hotel.

To reach the ashram in 1969, we had to take a five-
hour taxi ride over a broken, bumpy road that was paved
only part way and the last portion of the journey required
fording rivers. When the waters were too high, bullocks had
to be used to pull the taxi across. There was so much dust
in the car, even with the windows closed, that we had to
cover our noses and mouths with handkerchiefs. Our
fever-ridden bodies could not rest one moment as we were
constantly flying up and down, sometimes hitting the roof

of the car because of the deep potholes in the road. Time went slowly as I dreamt of the pleasure awaiting me: falling into bed in peace and quiet.

What a shock I got when we arrived! We were given one of the three guest rooms in the ashram: a dark cell with a concrete floor, completely bare. A smaller, adjoining room had a hole in the floor for a toilet but there was no running water or electricity. Unlike the ashram in the north, nothing was provided. Water to wash and flush the toilet had to be carried by bucket from a nearby well. Guests had to bring all the essentials such as mattresses, sheets and towels. Mother and I had brought only our personal belongings because the previous year mattresses had been provided to foreigners by the ashram.

Fortunately, someone had left two straw mats in the room: these did nothing by way of padding the concrete, but I appreciated anything to lie on as by that time I was delirious with fever. That night, I was awakened from a deep sleep by one loud bang after the another; they sounded like bombs and pierced my body like darts. Just outside our room, firecrackers were being lit one after the other for some celebration (I found out later that it was the Telugu New Year). This went on for hours and I kept muttering to my mother, "What kind of an ashram is this?"

For the next few days our fevers soared. We lay delirious, coughing constantly and finding no relief for our pain-racked bodies on the hard mats. Someone sent a doctor who gave us antibiotics, but still the fevers would not abate. Professor Kasturi (a long-time devotee of Sai Baba and author of many books about Him) came to our room to inform us that Sai Baba would see us in the morning for a private interview.

The following morning, still with high temperatures and dressed very inappropriately in our muumuus, we went to the interview. Sai Baba sat on the floor with us in a small room. He waved His palm in a circular motion and materialized a large piece of rock candy which He broke in two. Giving us each a piece He said, "The temperature will go." He turned to me and asked, "What do you want?" I could not think clearly, but obviously by my answer, what was uppermost in my mind was the welfare of animals. I could never bear to see them hurt and for years drove with my foot on the brake, ready to stop in case any creature ran out on the road. Since childhood, I have been totally identified with the suffering of any creature, and felt it would be a great relief if He could protect me from that pain. I answered, "Something to protect animals."

He asked, "Do you like my image?" I hesitated a moment before answering because, at that time, I did not particularly like His physical appearance. He certainly did not fit my concept of what a Holy Man should look like but how could I say this tactfully? So to be polite, I answered, "Yes." He again waved His palm in a circular motion and materialized a porcelain medallion which He handed to me. When I looked at the medallion, I was stunned to see a most unbecoming, out-of-proportion likeness of His face complete with a missing front tooth!

What to make of it all? So far, everything had shocked my expectations so severely, that had it not been for the fever numbing my mind, I might have felt totally unsound. But then Sai Baba waved His hand again and materialized for my mother a panchaloha ring on which was embossed His image with hand raised in blessing. (Panchaloha is composed of five different metals.) He inquired about my stepfather and other private matters and then, with great love and concern, He took my mother's hands in His and told her how very weak she was. He said we were both much too sick to come see Him again the next day. Instead, He added, He would come to our room to see us. Before the interview concluded, and to our surprise, He explained how beneficial tomato soup is for a fever. He added that it cools down the body and suggested we should have some. I was very moved by His love and concern and I could not remember having seen anyone bestow such superhuman love.

When we left the interview room, we both looked at each other and said, "Tomato soup!" How on earth were we going to find tomato soup here, we wondered. Puttaparthi, which was the place of Sai Baba's birth and location of his ashram, Prasanthi Nilayam (abode of the highest peace), was such a small village then, with only a few fruit and vegetable stands outside the ashram. Inside, the only food available was at a small canteen where very hot South Indian food was served on the floor, on banana leaves. The only silverware was your hands. One bite was enough to make our mouths burn so fiercely that eating such food was out of the question.

We soon dropped the idea of finding tomato soup as we had something more important to find, a chair. How could Sai Baba come to our dark, little room and not have a place to sit? As sick as we were, we busied ourselves borrowing items to furnish the room a bit; eventually we found a chair and a few more colorful mats. As we lay exhausted on our mats that evening, a kind lady staying in the other guest room offered us two bowls of tomato soup! We instantly recognized that her act had been divine inspiration. This tenderhearted lady had labored for hours peeling pounds of small tomatoes and then cooked them over a kerosene stove, on the floor, for two strangers. We had not eaten since we arrived and her soup proved to be the miracle prescription.

This kind lady was Mrs. Patel, the wife of Dr. G. Patel, who the previous year had been instrumental in Sai Baba's tour of East Africa. So far, this is the only location outside of India that Sai Baba has visited. We have remained friends with Mrs. Patel and often see her in the ashram on our yearly trip to India. She does not speak English but we usually have a good laugh when we meet because I always greet her with: "Tomato soup."

That evening, I thought about my first encounter with Sai Baba. I certainly was not one who recognized instantly His divinity as many claim to do. As I observed His every movement, gesture and expression throughout the interview, I knew I was not looking at a human being. I did not know what He was, but I knew what He was not. I realized after much deliberation that what I had not discerned in Sai Baba was the assertion of the ego: the human element. To see this is beyond description; it can only be experienced. The materializations were certainly amazing, but secondary. They were done in such an open, spontaneous and natural way that they left no question as to their authenticity. They undoubtedly were part of His nature as creation is an inseparable part of the creator. His super-human love, in itself, was the greatest miracle I had ever witnessed. It was so all encompassing, that when He focused it on me, the universe melted away and only He and I existed. Although it was not until the following year that He gave me the experience of an extraordinary state of bliss and an elevation of consciousness, for now at least, I knew I had found a great phenomenon and I hoped, my guru.

Sai Baba with my mother Jyothi Rajagopal. The name "Jyothi," was given to her by Sai Baba on her first trip.

SAI BABA MENDS A
BROKEN BONE

*Whenever your faith meets my love there is a
cure.*

Sathya Sai Baba

The next day as we sat in our room awaiting Sai
Baba, Professor Kasturi came to inform us that Sai Baba was
inviting us to the interview room to see Him since our health
had improved, and we were now able to walk more comfortably. My mother was still limping, and though our fevers
had gone entirely, we still felt pain throughout our bodies.

Sai Baba again sat on the floor with us. While He was
talking, I noticed that He lightly touched my mother's
broken toe for an instant. He told her she was very anemic
and then, quite suddenly, He materialized a pineapple-
shaped pendant covered with rubies. He told her that if
worn next to the skin it would help the anemia.

At one point, He took me to a separate area and
spoke privately for a full five minutes. He spoke so quickly,

with a suddenly assumed thick accent, that I could only grasp a few words here and there even though I was concentrating fully. I can read lips a little but He spoke too quickly for me to read His. At the time, I thought it must have been His accent. Now I know that this happens when He does not want you to understand, yet still wishes to give you the satisfaction of talking with Him. The more I discovered about Him, the more was left to discover. Deep introspection, trial and error and a desire to know the truth are the tools needed to begin understanding Sai Baba's mysterious ways, the sum total of which we can only hope to learn a very minuscule part.

The few words that I did understand suggested that I was working in a very bad atmosphere (I quit my job as soon as I returned) and that I should not be concerned about marital problems. The only question I asked Him was if the baby I was carrying would be all right, as I was concerned that my illness might affect the child. He assured me that the baby would be a healthy one. Those few words said by anyone else would have meant nothing but the moment Baba said them, they carried the power to completely lift the burden of worry from me. Though verbally they did not give an answer to my problems, the solution was to be found in my state of mind. He had transformed the inner self instead of the outer.

At the conclusion of the interview, we were deeply moved by Baba's love and concern when He offered us His car and driver to take us back to Bangalore. He said we were much too sick to stay in such an uncomfortable place and that we needed nourishing food and basic comforts to recuperate. Toward the end of the interview, He told us to come back for the celebration of His birthday.

We stood up as Sai Baba left the room. As we started to walk out, my mother let out a cry of delight upon discovering she was able to move her crippled toe: "Look, I can move my toe. It's fixed!" she exclaimed. I, too, was astounded at witnessing such a miracle. Even though I had seen Baba touch her toe, I never thought He could fix it or that He even knew it was broken as we hadn't told Him. I had naively categorized miracles as some being more difficult to perform than others. Omnipotence was a concept too complex for me to grasp at that point. Also, the manner in which He simply and gently touched her toe—without words or display of power—was surprising. I would have expected a certain amount of showy demonstration to emphasize such a miracle. How many false concepts I had to eliminate! How many opinions and ideas had been formed erroneously throughout my life! The spiritual path has been, and continues to be for me, a purifier of the mind.

Back at the West End Hotel in Bangalore, we had all the comforts and were able to get our much needed rest. We still had difficulty eating as the food made us ill. How well I understood the saying, "Man does not live by bread alone." Having just experienced the ashram atmosphere, I was now aware, that in spite of all the food and comforts I had always had, I was spiritually starved. The hard floor and Mrs. Patel's tomato soup were much more valuable than soft beds and banquets because of Sai Baba's love.

After Mother and I had recuperated somewhat, we decided to hire a taxi and explore the sights of Bangalore. There were not many interesting things to see and we quickly tired. The driver must have sensed our desire to return to the hotel because just as we were about to tell him, he told us he wanted to show us a wonderful thing. He turned the car around and explained that he was taking us to see a great yogi and self-realized man. He then took us to a very small house where many disciples had gathered. They were walking around a cot on which the yogi was lying and would take turns bowing down to him and touching his feet. The eyes of the yogi were dull and he had a body like a hippopotamus. Inside the house the atmosphere was dreary and dark; we felt such a repulsion that we quickly left the place.

After seeing the sun (Baba), the yogi appeared as small as a firefly and he was the last yogi or guru that I have gone out of my way to see. Just as a happily married woman does not look at other men, I have never felt the need or had the curiosity to see another guru. I have always believed that loyalty is essential in the worldly as well as the spiritual life.

The beggars in India caused me much distress; I had never seen so many people in such a pitiful condition. I felt such pain just looking at them. There were lepers with missing pieces of flesh; partially paralyzed beggars crawled on all fours in the filthy streets and there were mutilated children without limbs. But I could not help them all and if I gave money to one, swarms of others would gather with outstretched hands and pitiful pleas. I did have the satisfaction of meeting one most unusual, elderly beggar on Commercial Street. He spoke English and had a great sense of humor in spite of being without a leg. He never begged like the others but waited to be given a small compensation for performing any service he could, such as opening the car door or carrying a package. I grew very fond of him, and it gave me great pleasure to offer him something when we met. I was grateful that through him, I was —at least in a small way— able to satisfy my desire to help beggars.

Listen to the primeval Pranava AUM resounding in your heart as well as in the heart of the Universe.

Sathya Sai Baba

OUR LAST DARSHAN

Man lives by getting and forgetting. God lives by giving and forgiving.

Sathya Sai Baba

We returned to Prasanthi Nilayam for Sai Baba's birthday. He tenderly greeted us among the thousands of people gathered, saying: "So you have come, bangaru." (Bangaru is an endearing word which means "gold.") The expression made us feel welcomed and loved. We witnessed a beautiful celebration which included Baba's mother applying oil to His hair. After the talks, He fed each person assembled prasad (blessed food) on a banana leaf. His gown was drenched with perspiration and watching Him bend down thousands of times to serve each one in the sweltering, humid heat was a torment. I am sure many devotees were in anguish and praying to Him to stop as we were; we just could not endure seeing Him labor so strenuously.

In later years, He did stop the feeding as the masses grew to hundreds of thousands but never did He stop giving. His very nature is expansive, selfless, always giving.

His healing rays of love refresh the troubled, the sick and the lost. His hands constantly distribute saris, shirts, dhotis (long cloth worn as a covering by men), pencils to students, sweets to the workers, the poor and His devotees. He always gives a personal touch to festivals and special celebrations by distributing gifts personally and showering His motherly love on devotees.

While He was distributing large stacks of saris to the poor, I noticed how carefully He chose the color each lady preferred. Sometimes, He would tease them by handing them a color they obviously did not like, but before they could say, "thank you" or touch His feet in gratitude, He would quickly take it back and give them the color they preferred. The expression of delight and tears in the eyes of these ladies would tell the story. We were among the doubly delighted that year when He gave Mother and me two beautiful silk saris to wear for the birthday celebration.

After many hours, we started feeling weak and faint from a combination of intense heat and being tightly pressed against each other in spite of being seated in the front as guests. Our squatting on the ground and the lack of fresh air were becoming physically unbearable. So in the evening before our endurance wore out completely we took a taxi back to Bangalore as our departure date was fast approaching.

The evening before we left Bangalore, I suddenly remembered my beggar friend. Thinking we might not return to India for a long time, Mother and I jumped out of bed, put on raincoats over our nightgowns and took a taxi to Commercial Street to give our friend a goodbye present. After twenty years, I still make a special trip to Commercial Street to find my friend whenever I visit Bangalore. He is all grey now and with no teeth, but as sweet and helpful as ever.

Our first stop on our return journey was Italy our homeland and land of our very favorite food. We were so starved for rich, familiar food that we had carefully planned the menu and dreamed of the mouth-watering goodies awaiting us. We asked for such strange mixtures of food that the waiter was puzzled as he repeated the order for confirmation. He must have thought we were two uncultured ladies who did not even know the basic food combinations. Our mouths watered until the food arrived, but as we started to eat we experienced an overpowering feeling of nausea which was so acute that we could not bear to even look at the remainder of the food.

Our round-the-world ticket was also a waste. We had made plans to stop in several countries that we had never visited and wanted so much to see. We had ample time but were too sick to enjoy ourselves. So we canceled all our reservations and returned directly home.

This has continued for the past twenty years. For some reason or other I am not able to enjoy a vacation. Now, when time is available, I have lost all desire to go anywhere but to India. In part, I feel that distractions are placed before me to test my commitment. Is the spiritual path of uppermost importance or is the world still of primary interest? I now know that when going to see Baba all of my energy and attention must be focused on the one goal; otherwise, they are frivolously dispersed and wasted. "Time waste is life waste" says Baba. A growing awareness of how much time is needlessly wasted in my life has caused numerous desires to drop away naturally and without struggle.

Sai Baba with author, Joel and Christina in Brindavan.

THAT CHARACTER

*Education is a slow process like the unfolding
of a flower: the fragrance becoming deeper and
more perceptible with the silent blossoming,
petal by petal, of the entire flower.*

Sathya Sai Baba

Upon my return, I spoke most enthusiastically
about Sai Baba to my husband, Joel. I hoped that if I could
only get him interested, perhaps all our difficulties could be
resolved. I began by displaying pictures of Baba in the
house and bringing books about Him for Joel to read. When
I told him of the materializations I had witnessed, Joel was
sure they were tricks. Having worked on stage with
magicians and knowing well how illusions are created, he
felt he could easily prove to me they were tricks and show
me how they were done. Even my mother's broken toe he
explained away to his own satisfaction. I realized that
patience was needed in order to convince Joel. This was an
important issue and forcefulness on my part would be
counterproductive.

When his friends came to visit, Joel would tell me to remove "that character's" picture. He always referred to Baba as "that character." I could not interest him, but I noticed that the more opposition I got the stronger my faith grew.

After the birth of our daughter, Christina, Joel's business crumbled. He tried desperately to save it but failed. His friends slowly dropped away and life began to weigh heavily upon him.

I showed him a book on Sai Baba by Arnold Schulman. It aroused his interest because Schulman was a playwright and his kind of person and not, he felt, a religious fanatic. He started thinking there might be some truth to it. He began to show Schulman's book to friends and explain how "this character" materializes things out of the air and how much fun it would be to see him perform. When his friends asked Joel what he would ask the "character" to materialize for him, he replied, "a rainbow." A rainbow could not be brought out from inside the sleeve and it would prove Baba was genuine. But, Joel added, the main reason for going to India to see Him was to show his wife what a fool she was to fall for this trickster.

THE RAINBOW

*You ask from Me a thousand things of the
world, but rarely do you ask for Me.*

Sathya Sai Baba

Christina was a year and a half old when we left
for India. Up to the last minute Joel kept changing his mind
and that kept me in a state of suspense until we finally
boarded the plane; only then did I feel secure. When we
arrived at the ashram, Joel was appalled at the primitive
living conditions and grumbled endlessly while we unloaded our luggage. My mother had been in the ashram for
a month before we arrived, and as rooms were scarce we
shared a room with her. We came well supplied from
Bangalore with food, mattresses and everything needed to
soften and pamper our spoiled western bodies. I was happy
and serene but could see Joel's tension mounting; it needed
an outlet. Smoking is not allowed in the ashram so I took
him to the hills behind our room, outside the boundaries, to
have a smoke.

We sat on a large rock and looked at the view of the
valley of Puttaparthi in the late afternoon; it was mag-

nificent. We could see for miles and follow the river below, winding through the peaceful valley surrounded by mountains and deep silence. Suddenly, Joel looked up at the sky and exclaimed, full of wonder and surprise, "Look, look at the rainbow!" I looked up and saw a most peculiar rainbow. It was not curved, but went straight up in the sky and started dissolving slowly from the bottom up while I was looking at it. "What is so interesting about that?" I asked him. "Don't you remember? That is what I wanted to ask Sai Baba to make for me, a rainbow!" Joel answered a bit shaken. I did not reply because I thought Joel's request was absurd. Why should Baba take the trouble to make him a rainbow? Not that I thought He couldn't make one, but why make such a big thing for such a skeptic? I did not tell Joel my thoughts. I wanted him to believe but strangely enough I did not. Joel looked all around the sky and noticed there were no clouds; it was a perfectly clear day. We had just arrived and not spoken to anyone, so he discarded the possibility that someone could have told Baba that he wanted a rainbow. Only his friends in Los Angeles knew.

When we returned to the room, Professor Kasturi greeted us with the wonderful news that Sai Baba had called us for an interview the following morning.

In the morning, we waited in the interview room for Sai Baba to come downstairs. Joel was standing at the foot of the stairs and as Baba reached the bottom, He turned to Joel with a big smile and said, "Well, character, how did you like my rainbow?" as He slapped Joel affectionately on the back.

Joel stood speechless, as if frozen, while tears came to his eyes and rolled down his cheeks. Tears and shame overcame me as well when I realized I was in no position to judge if a person's request was silly, or how deserving anyone is of Baba's grace and love. There is no difference for Baba in making a ring or a rainbow. Nor can any of His manifestations be labeled as "big" or "small," or require "more" or "less" trouble for Him. All of these labels are based on our misconceptions.

Sai Baba sat on a chair and we gathered around Him on the floor; Joel sat at the foot of His chair. Baba turned to a lady from Mexico and said, "Your knees have been hurting you." She nodded. Baba glanced at Joel before He carefully pulled up His sleeve as far as it would go (He often does this for skeptics), and waved His hand in a circular motion. When He turned it upwards there appeared on the palm of His hand, vibhuti, which He gave to the lady from Mexico. He then turned to me and asked how my daughter was feeling. I replied, "Not very well." She had a cold and intestinal problems. He again waved His hand and materialized a fresh fig which He told me to give to Christina. The atmosphere was joyous and electric as Baba talked and joked with all of us. During that hour, time stood still and could not be counted. Each moment was eternal. No experience, even the most thrilling I could recall, could compare to the joy of being in His presence. I was beginning to experience a blissful state which grew in intensity as time passed.

When we left the interview room, Joel immediately started his investigation of the fig Baba had materialized. He went to the little village just outside the ashram to see if they were selling figs. He was told that it was not the season for figs; not a single fresh fig could be found anywhere in South India!

Joel told me that when we were in the interview room he was wishing Baba would materialize a fruit the very moment before He did. He had carefully watched Baba's hands during the materializations and could not detect trickery. Baba had taken him aside for a few moments and privately told Joel things about his life that no one knew and that Joel was not thinking about at the time. Mind reading was out. Joel was becoming fascinated with his "character."

Joel was also becoming fascinated with the low cost of living in India. With a few hundred dollars a month, one could live like a king in royal style. Western-style homes only cost a few thousand dollars. He started talking to landowners who were selling land outside the ashram, looking at parcels, talking to contractors and gathering as much information as he could. I could see he was seriously considering staying in India. We had seen Baba privately in several other interviews, in which He discouraged Joel, saying Puttaparthi was not the right place to buy land.

We engaged a village girl to help me look after Christina, draw water from the well and clean our room. The girl was not much help with Christina except for playing with her. She did not speak a word of English and was afraid of safety pins so she could not even change diapers. She looked frightening with long teeth that protruded straight out of her mouth like fangs. When Christina was not distracted by play, she often stared at the girl with an expression suggesting that at any moment she could burst into tears.

Every day the girl would perform a strange ceremony. She would wave her hand, full of salt and chili peppers, many times around Christina's body. She ended the ritual by pouring yellow liquid on Christina's head. The first time I saw her pouring the smelly liquid, I tried to stop her, but she silently and solemnly motioned me out of the way. I searched out the resident doctor who had recommended the girl to me, to inquire about the meaning of this act.

The doctor explained that this was the evil eye ceremony. Many Indians perform this ritual daily as it has the power to remove the subtle influence left in our aura by people's thoughts. Whatever people think when looking at us affects and stays with us. If these subtle thoughts are many and strong, they accumulate and ultimately affect our gross part, the body, causing health to deteriorate. I have had many occasions to test the efficacy of this theory and found amazing results using salt alone. I never experimented with the liquid though; it was cow urine!

Our being in the ashram and Joel's developing interest in Sai Baba did not resolve our marital problems or strengthen our marriage as I thought it would. We were still arguing and had even more disagreements. The strenuous living conditions caused more tension than ever. Very soon our food supply was reduced to peanut butter and rice. The disposable diapers had run out and Christina had constant diarrhea. I had no sleep from being up all night caring for her, and to worsen the situation, there was no water available to rinse and soak the soiled diapers. Joel was oblivious to my nighttime activity and worry since he moved his cot outside on the porch, and slept peacefully throughout the night. In desperation I pleaded with Joel to take turns staying up with the baby, but he coldly and flatly refused. I was exhausted and my nerves were strained to their limits.

The morning following our argument, Sai Baba called us for an interview. Once in the interview room, I could not hold back the tears. Swami (by now I addressed Him as His devotees did) was more loving and consoling than any mother could possibly have been. The love that poured from Him was so moving that I cried even more.

I felt confused and wanting so much to see clearly, I asked Swami how to distinguish right from wrong. He knew I was not in a position to look within as I had not yet developed self-confidence so, like a mother assuming responsibility for her child until it matures, He lovingly assured me that whenever I prayed to him—within half an hour—He would always give an answer. Through the years He has kept that promise to me. With this beautiful promise and loving assurance, tears started flowing again.

Swami quickly distracted me. As though waving a rattle to a baby, He waved His hand and materialized an exquisite pair of clip earrings (pearls surrounded by three rows of sparkling diamonds). Before giving them to me, He placed them on His own ears and moved back His hair so we could admire them. Looking at Swami with the earrings, I felt transported back in time, thousands of years, to the epoch of the Krishna Avatar (Krishna is pictured as being decorated with various jewels); I felt I had a glimpse of the breathtakingly exquisite beauty ascribed to Lord Krishna. Swami later removed the earrings and placed them delicately on my ears as I knelt at His feet. Turning to Joel, Swami asked: "Jealous?" "No," Joel replied. I knew he was not and a year later learned that Swami's comment was indirectly intended for a girl present, who confessed how terribly jealous she felt when I received the earrings. She knew

Swami had directed the question to Joel so as not to expose her feelings because she would have been mortified.

As soon as we left the interview room, Joel took one of my earrings and bit the pearl to see if it was real; I was furious. My consciousness was immediately lowered as I expressed anger at his ability to spoil my most beautiful moments with Swami. I was also angry with myself for reacting in such an immature manner. It took seven years of practice before I learned to be indifferent to Joel's opinions and actions. Looking back, I see that I should have been grateful instead of grumbling about my fate as our greatest difficulties are always our best teachers.

Camp.
"Brindavan"

My Dear Rajagopal! Accept my Love and Blessings

By your discretion convert All stumbling blocks of the world into stepping stones to realisation.

The energy we waste in judging others is just what is need to make us live up to our own ideals.

Assert your GOD-head Fling into utter oblivion the little self, as if it had never existed. when the little bubble bursts, it finds itself the whole ocean. You are the whole, the Infinite, the All.

Dear Raju! out of long churning this milk of the world comes butter and this butter is GOD. Men of heart get the butter, and the butter-Milk is left for the intellectual.

Aim at a lion and miss it; rather than hunt a jackal and catch it.

Let GOD work through you, and there will be no more duty. Let GOD shine forth. Let GOD show Himself. Realise the Truth and the other things will take care of themselves.

Raju! don't worry, Be happy Swamiji is always with you. in you jyoti is very good girl make happy and give Santosh,

With Love
Baba

Several of the letters that Sai Baba has written to my stepfather have been reproduced throughout this book. When asking permission to print them, Sai Baba requested that the personal passages be deleted. This has been done.

A SURPRISE GIFT

*The body is a house given to you for rent; the
owner is God. Live there so long as He wills,
thanking Him and paying Him the rent of
faith and devotion.*

Sathya Sai Baba

After about one month, Swami went to Brindavan,
His residence near Whitefield which is a half-hour drive
from Bangalore. Joel was delighted to be back at the West
End Hotel. The comforts and good food improved his
humor and the daily taxi rides back and forth were a
pleasant distraction. Early in the morning, we would take a
taxi to Swami's house and stay there until lunchtime. When
we were not invited to lunch with Swami, we went back to
the hotel until about four, returned and stayed in Brindavan
until about eight in the evening.

Swami lived in an old two-story house on a ten-acre
compound, surrounded entirely by a high, stone wall. The
property was further divided by another wall that separated
His private residence from the public area. Here visitors and

devotees would gather twice a day in orderly rows waiting for Him to give darshan (the sight of a great being).

As He walked amongst the crowd, He chose people for private interview and the persons chosen would be led by a volunteer to Swami's house. There were always guests, which included Joel and me, who were invited to sit (men on one side and women on the other) in the main room the entire day. Swami's chair was almost in the middle of the division between the men and women. Sometimes, the people He chose for interview would be seen by Swami in another room, but often He would invite them into the main room and we could witness and take part in the interview.

Usually when Swami invited guests to sit in the main room, they would enter the grounds from the private, back gate instead of the front. The invitation was valid only for the duration of their visit. A new invitation had to be received from Swami when one returned to India. Many people found themselves embarrassed because they would not be allowed in the house on their next visit. We soon learned that it was up to us to investigate and discover what the unspoken rules were, or we were bound to suffer the consequences of our ignorance. One learns quickly not to take Swami for granted.

His presence commands the utmost respect. One does not speak unless spoken to, but waits patiently for the right moment and Swami's indication before asking a question. The highest etiquette is always followed by His closest devotees, and we had to find out what that entailed in Indian customs so as not to make mistakes. All are silent yet very alert, ready to act and react their very best to the many unexpected events that happen throughout the day. We had to be heedful of our thoughts as we knew that Swami is aware of every thought that comes into our minds, often exposing them to teach us awareness and introspection. The discipline of sitting silently for hours and practicing awareness, was an incredible training that I did not fully appreciate at the time, as I was often restless and in great discomfort from sitting in silence on the hard floor the entire day.

When Swami was with us in the main room, we were in heaven; all tension, pain and restlessness vanished instantly. Watching Him was a delight to the eye. Hearing Him was food for the soul. Does there exist a human being on earth that one would not tire of looking at? We drank in Swami's beauty with an unquenchable thirst. His every movement is pure grace, putting to shame the greatest of dancers. His smile lights the room and brings unsurpassed joy to our hearts. His unmatched humor brings peals of laughter and delight, transforming us into little children. His wisdom is so profound, that with a few simple words, we not only understand but experience truth. His beauty Divine, is almost liquid in its ability to change from the delicately feminine to the strongest masculine appearance. Even the color of His skin changes from the lightest ivory to the darkest brown. What a wonder to watch this continuous transformation, this heavenly phenomenon!

I often asked myself when I looked at Him, Who is He? Can the omnipresent God be contained in a human body? Why not choose a form more in keeping with humanity's concept of God? And there were so many other questions.

Looking back, I marvel at how patiently He dissolved my doubts and answered all my questions. I see why He had to go slowly, waiting for me to mature so I could understand His answers. Just as a fruit cannot be ripened artificially, He could not give me instant maturity and understanding defying the laws of evolution.

Joel was also having many baffling experiences that created puzzling questions and doubts in his mind. But as he had never studied books or religious scriptures, his conclusions were often very strange. He could never accept the fact that God could assume a human form, but felt that Swami was possibly a rare human who had somehow developed His potential to a maximum level. But then, most likely He was an alien from another planet, he conjectured. Of course the idea that Swami was a Martian irritated me no end and caused endless arguments between us.

One morning Swami went outside, and while putting on His sandals (He is always barefoot unless He goes on rough terrain) asked us to follow Him. Dr. John (Jack) Hislop, his wife Victoria, and my mother were also there and joined us as we walked behind Swami. The land behind His house was bare except for a few cowsheds and a house under construction. He led us to the house and slowly through each partially erected room, all the while explaining what each room would become. Joel saw a very small room and assumed it would be a closet but when he asked, Swami jokingly replied it was an Indian-style kitchen.

While we were walking back to Swami's house, He turned to Joel and asked: "Do you like the house?" "Oh yes!" said Joel. "It's yours," Swami stated. We were all taken by surprise. After a long pause Joel asked, "Swami, is this a joke?" "No, no joke. It's yours," Swami assured him. We had to use some control in order not to jump for joy at the thought of living in a house right next to Swami. What a monumental gift He gave us! After about one year, Swami built two more houses next to ours. One was given to Dr. Hislop and the other to Mrs. Brij Ratanlal, the lady with whom I had shared a taxi on my first visit to Swami. For many years she was in charge of the Brindavan Press which printed the monthly magazine, "Sanathana Sarathi." She also had the unique blessing to be personally trained by Swami in South Indian cooking, and she often cooked for Swami and His guests.

Swami later introduced us to the builder, and asked us to discuss with him any changes we wished to make while construction was still in progress. It was a large house: two bedrooms, two bathrooms, a large living room, kitchen and two porches. Since Swami had designated what the rooms were to be, we decided not to make any major changes. We debated a long time over the joke about the closet; we could not possibly make it into a kitchen as it was so small. We wondered what He had meant because we knew that every word He said had a deeper significance. Sometimes, with introspection, one can discover the meaning quickly; other times only years later one understands. Swami told us that when the house was finished, He would arrange a house opening. In India, it is the custom never to move into a new home without a proper ceremony.

Sai Baba with author and Joel on the occasion of their house opening in Brindavan. Story page 59.

VANQUISHED FEAR

*Do not be like the gramophone records singing
someone else's song, ignorant of the genuine
thrill of music. Sing from your own experience of the glory and grace of the Lord.*

Sathya Sai Baba

Swami invited my family and the Hislops to join
Him on a trip to Madras where He would be presiding over
the All-India Conference in December 1971. I observed from
the very beginning, that whenever any event is organized
by Swami, He supervises and personally sees to every
minute detail.

During a month-long summer course, an enormous
amount of work must be done: tents are erected, kitchens
to feed hundreds are set up, living quarters are arranged,
speakers must be picked up at the airport. During this time,
Swami sees streams of people and meticulously goes over
every detail with each one. On this occasion, I observed
Swami taking time from this superhuman schedule to go to
His dog kennel and remind the boys in charge of the dogs
that they had forgotten to feed the animals.

In the same way, Swami carefully saw to every detail of the preparations for our trip to Madras: the kinds of food to be taken, accommodations in Madras for His guests, the number of cars and who would occupy them. He did all this in addition to making preparations for the many thousands who were expected to attend the conference.

It was necessary to take an ayah (nanny) with me to care for Christina, or else I could not have attended the conference. We had to instruct her and our driver not to breathe a word of our travel plans. Whenever Swami travels, the plans have to be kept absolutely secret; otherwise, hundreds of people would follow, crowd around Him should He stop and disrupt the entire journey. There is also the danger of drivers competing recklessly in order to get closest to Swami's car. Even though the official rule is that one cannot follow Swami without His permission, people often break the rule and justify it with the much abused expression, "It's God's will."

Fortunately on this trip plans were not revealed and no one followed. Consequently, about a half hour out of Bangalore, Swami was able to stop His car and invite Mrs. Hislop, Mother and me to sit in the back seat of His Impala station wagon. Swami sat in the front seat next to Professor V.K. Gokak (the former vice-chancellor of Baba's university).

The hours that followed on my first trip in the car with Swami were most memorable. The atmosphere was electrifying; every moment was charged with pure joy. Swami asked us if we wanted Him to sing a bhajan (devotional song). Before I came to India, I had heard a recording of Swami's singing "Govinda Krishna Jai." I loved His voice and that bhajan so much that my continuous playing of the record soon wore it out. I immediately jumped at the opportunity of hearing Him sing in person this very beautiful song; I told Him my request. As He sang my favorite bhajan, His angelic, melodious voice sent a heavenly thrill through me; time was suspended, paradise could not be anywhere other than where I was at that moment.

Upon finishing the song, He asked us to sing. Mrs. Hislop knew only one bhajan which she bravely sang. Swami interrupted the singing a few times to correct her pronunciation. Then He asked me to sing and I was overcome by fear, panic and dread. I could not answer. Public singing had always been impossible for me; I could only sing if I were alone. Therefore, no one had ever heard me. If I tried to sing before anyone, fear paralyzed my vocal cords and not a sound would come out.

With some courage I stammered a reply: "I cannot sing, Swami." "Yes you can," He affirmed. "I don't have a voice," I replied. "Everybody has a voice," He reminded me with a laugh. "But I don't know any bhajans," I pleaded, hoping to escape His request. "You know other songs," He coaxed. My mind was thoroughly blank; I could not think of a single song. My dear mother was quick to help and suggested the Christmas song, "Silent Night." Now I was cornered. I shuddered and trembled, knowing the time had come to face this fear, and somehow mustered up the courage necessary to sing "Silent Night." I was even able to reach the high notes of the concluding phrase—"Sleep in heavenly peace"—without squeaking. When I finished, Swami turned to Professor Gokak and said, "Beautiful." As of that moment, my fear and complex vanished. Only a person who has experienced such paralyzing fear can understand the gratitude and relief I felt for what Swami had done for me. I was astonished by the exhilaration one experiences when fears are faced and overcome. Now, when I am happy, I can express it by singing to my heart's content.

For a long time in the car, Swami talked to us about His childhood with Professor Gokak translating. He told us many stories that have never been made public, about the hardships He endured as a young boy before revealing His Divinity. We listened with rapt attention—tears in our eyes—at the bravery and silence kept by the young Sathya.

The mood quickly changed when Swami spotted a secluded place off the main road and signaled the driver to stop for a picnic. Blankets were spread and tiffin carriers unloaded under Swami's directions. He carefully inspected the food being placed on each plate before He handed it to us. He would joke and make us laugh (all the while keeping a watchful eye on our plates). If any of us ate a particular portion with gusto, He would immediately order a second helping to be brought to us. If we did not eat something, He wanted to know why. Did we not like it? Was it fattening or not digestible? What an example Swami was as to how we should be: always concerned about the welfare of others, always giving. His keen power of observation continually searched out ways to benefit others and to express love to each and every person and creature. I have seen Swami go out of His way, while distributing prasad (blessed food), to make sure that even a stray dog wandering near by would get its portion. Before reaching Madras, we all returned to our original places in the various cars.

A RESURRECTION

*You have been born for one purpose: To die.
That is to say, to kill the "I." All this literature,
all this effort, all this yagna (spiritual exercise), all this teaching is just to hold a mirror
before you, so that you may see yourself.*

Sathya Sai Baba

In Madras, Swami stayed at the house of an old
devotee, Sushilamma, while we were accommodated in the
guest house of a recent devotee, Mr. Sathuraman. The guest
house was enchanting. Tame deer and peacocks roamed
freely in the lush, tropical gardens. A full staff of servants
were at our disposal and responded to our every need. An
excellent cook made us delicious vegetarian meals. I was
happy to leave Christina and the ayah in this lovely surrounding while we went with Swami to visit various homes
of His devotees and attend the conference.

Our host, Mr. Sathuraman, was a great devotee of
Lord Ganesha (the Indian god with the elephant head and
known as the remover of obstacles). He presented each of
us staying at his guest house with the gift of a statue of

Ganesha. In later years, he donated a life-size statue of Ganesha to the ashram and it is installed at the front gate. To this day, the statue has been an inspiration for thousands of visitors and residents and is worshiped daily, according to tradition, by the pundits.

Swami invited us to dine with Him at the home of the Indian actress, Anjali Devi. Near here was a vacant parcel of land on which in later years was erected "Sundaram," Swami's residence when He visits Madras. After dinner, we all enjoyed a preview of her latest film but did not see the end as Swami was concerned with giving darshan to the hundreds of people gathered outside the house. Thus, the film was cut short as He responded to the longing in the hearts of His devotees.

On December 25, 1971 while giving a discourse, Swami suddenly stopped speaking, walked over to Dr. Jack Hislop at the side of the stage and whispered something to him. Jack left immediately and Swami resumed the discourse. When we returned to the guest house, Dr. Hislop told us a fascinating story. Swami had told him that Walter Cowan had just died and that Elsie, his wife, was at that moment fervently praying and calling Swami. He told Jack to go to Mrs. Cowan and assure her that He had heard her prayer and would soon be coming to the hospital to see Walter.

Elsie and Walter Cowan, founders of the Sathya Sai Book Center of America, had arrived a few days earlier from the United States and were staying in a hotel in Madras. That morning, Mr. Cowan had died in his wife's arms. An ambulance was called, and his body was taken to a hospital and placed in a storage room after being pronounced dead.

Swami visited the hospital later and restored life to the body of Walter Cowan.

A month later, in Brindavan, Walter Cowan told me of his experience with death. He said that shortly after he died, he remained near his physical body in the ambulance. Then the scene suddenly changed. Swami came and took him to a large room, somewhere in the heavens, where a panel of judges were gathered. He was shown scenes from many of his past lives where he recognized himself as having been, very often, a person of great historic importance. He saw that, throughout these lives, he had always worked for the welfare of humanity. After the lives appeared before Walter, Swami told the panel of judges that He was taking him back to Earth because there was still work to be done by Mr. Cowan. Walter told me he was not happy to come back, as being without a body gave him an enormous sensation of expansive freedom.

Sai Baba with Elsie and Walter Cowan on the occasion of their remarriage. Story page 59.

Sai Baba with author and Joel in Brindavan.

AMRITA, THE NECTAR OF IMMORTALITY

Man can be certified as healthy, only when he is fully conscious of his reality and is gladly striving to reach it. Now, he is the child of Immortality.

Sathya Sai Baba

On January first, a few days after we returned to Brindavan from Madras, Swami told us to have our cars ready as that evening He was taking us and the Kamani family to the riverbed.

The Kamani family was headed by several brothers who were owners of large steel factories in India; they were greatly devoted to Swami. We came to know well the eldest, Poornachandra and his wife Sumitra, and found them to be supreme examples of devotees capable of balancing the life of the world with that of the spirit. They practiced having their "hands in society and head in the forest," as Swami teaches.

Swami asked Colonel Jogarao that afternoon to find a pleasant spot on the riverbed. That evening, the brightest full moon was shining as we followed Swami's car to a spot chosen beforehand by the Colonel. As he showed Swami the spot he picked, Swami commented that there was not much sand but He would manage. We wondered why He needed sand and could not imagine what He was planning to do, or why He had brought us here. The constant anticipation of the unexpected makes being with Swami a great adventure.

We sat in a circle around Swami and watched as He started playing with the sand. First, He flattened and patted the sand, making a smooth foundation. Next, He gathered more sand and made a mound on top of the flat surface. Then, He carefully drew a design on the very top of the mound. Looking at us with a mischievous smile, He reached just below the design and pulled out a little brass urn. We all gasped in astonishment. "Amrita," Swami said.

Amrita is the fabled nectar that gives immortality which according to the Indian scriptures was first obtained by churning the ocean of milk. Swami tried to open the screw top, but it was difficult. "Tight fit," He said as He tried a second time and succeeded. He then asked if anyone had a spoon. Some of the men jumped up and scurried about but could not find one. Swami waved His hand in large circular motions and immediately we saw the hand grasping a spoon. He asked for a cup into which He poured all the amrita from the urn.

The college boys started singing bhajans. Their celestial voices and sound of the drums created a heavenly atmosphere as Swami walked down the line pouring spoonfuls of amrita into our mouths. The taste of the divine nectar was indescribable: a mixture of honey, roses and delicate spices. That moment was divinely sweet and sacred as though filled with celestial music.

Next, Swami gave Joel the cup and asked him to pour the remaining amrita back into the urn. Joel was astounded to find the amrita filled the urn to the very top!

Once again, we sat down on the sand around Swami as He started to smooth and pat the sand as He had done before. We watched eagerly for the next wonder to emerge. He took an unusually long time drawing every little detail. When He reached into the sand this time, He had to use both hands to pull out a large gold statue of the Indian god Rama together with Sita, Lakshmana and Hanuman. We crowded around to get a closer look at the magnificent creation which Swami later presented to Sumitra and Poornachandra Kamani for placement on their altar for puja (worship).

On the ride back to Brindavan, I was in a most blissful state, feeling grateful to have started the New Year in such an auspicious way and wanted to preserve the sacredness with silence. I had no idea, at the time, that what I witnessed had a much deeper and mystical significance.

Swami had told Poornachandra Kamani to begin preparations for his retirement and free himself from all responsibilities, as he would be spending the remainder of his life with Swami in Prasanthi Nilayam.

Only Swami knew, on New Year's Day of 1972, the significance of the nectar of immortality He had given to Mr. Kamani, as He alone was aware of his destiny and future plan (that would occur in only a few months) to immortalize the memory and name of this dear devotee.

Poornachandra, after receiving the sacred amrita, had returned to Bombay and followed Swami's instructions. His last task was to turn the business over to his brothers in a farewell speech to the board of directors of the company. As he concluded the meeting by thanking his staff and asking the board members to give the same love and support to his brothers which they had given him—so that now he could join his beloved Guru—he collapsed into the arms of his wife and never regained consciousness.

The Governor of Karnataka State was in Prasanthi Nilayam with Swami when this occurred and witnessed His omniscience when Swami lovingly placed His hand on His heart and said, "Kamani has come."

Only five days after his passing, Swami immortalized his name by naming the auditorium in Prasanthi Nilayam, Poornachandra, in honor of the man who donated the hall and undoubtedly is spending his retirement in the abode of the highest peace.

> *Becoming immortal does not imply that one can avoid death and continue living in the physical body for all time. It means only that his name and fame will shine in the memories of people. When your deeds are holy, coming generations will emulate them and offer gratitude for the example.*
>
> Sathya Sai Baba

THE HOUSE OPENING

I bring tears of joy into your eyes and I wipe the tears of grief.

Sathya Sai Baba

The time for the house opening had arrived. Fortunately, Swami gave us a few days' notice; often one is not given advance notice as He teaches us to be always ready for the unexpected and to flow with life calmly while using our minds quickly in making the right decisions. By watching ourselves and our reactions, we become aware of how little and how slowly we learn.

My mother had made inquiries among the Indian ladies as to what we were expected to bring to the house opening. They informed her that we should buy fruit to be distributed later as prasad, and a garland of fresh flowers because on such occasions Swami is given a garland. In India it is the custom for devotees to bring flowers or fruit to the guru, so at the front gate of the compound they were always available for purchase.

Mother would not hear of buying Swami an ordinary garland from the vendors at the front gate; she wanted the very best for Him. She always put forth maximum effort in doing whatever she felt would please Swami the most. She was amazingly quick to grasp a hint from Him and learned at lightning speed. She has been, and continues to be, my most reliable guide for understanding the ways and wishes of Swami. At the same time, I realize that I am much slower to learn than she and not nearly as intuitive. We went to the central market in Bangalore and spent much time examining the various flowers until Mother found the very best roses. We ordered a magnificent, thick, five-foot-long garland of mixed colors.

On the morning of the house opening, Swami gave my mother and me each a splendid sari and told us to put them on; we went to another room and changed. Attired in our new saris, we followed Swami outside, where, to our surprise was assembled an entire band. The band started playing grandly and beating the drums full force as we all walked in procession towards the new house. In the group, there were many foreigners including Joel's favorite, Arnold Schulman, whom Swami had invited for this occasion. Upon looking around at the crowd, I began feeling a bit anxious; I had not expected such an impressive affair.

We followed Swami into the house which had been tastefully decorated with carpets, flowers, oil lamps, a large picture of Swami and His chair. When the group had gathered inside, I glanced at Swami to see what I should do. He motioned for me to go over to an oil lamp and I understood I should light it and looked around for matches. I found them and attempted to light one, but my hands trembled making it impossible. I looked to Swami for help.

He immediately responded by coming to me; He took the matches from my shaking hand and lit the lamp Himself. Dear Swami, Lord of the Universe, yet always there rushing to help with our petty little difficulties.

We sat cross-legged on the carpet and sang bhajans for sometime. At the conclusion of bhajans, a bucket of homemade amrita was brought to me together with a spoon. Swami directed me to distribute the nectar to those present. I concluded it should be poured into people's mouths as Swami had done at the riverbed, but when I proceeded to do so, a kind Indian lady directed me to put the amrita in the palms of the hands.

Swami then presented us with several gifts for our house opening: a tray on wheels (He had earlier suggested we should have one upon visiting the house because the kitchen was very long), a chair for Swami and a beautiful picture of Himself that Joel had admired previously when it hung in the main room of Swami's house. We now followed Swami to the front porch where the garland of roses was lying in a covered basket. I then placed the beautiful garland upon Swami's shoulders and noticed that it almost touched the ground. Immediately after, Swami waved His hand and materialized two rings. One, He gave to me and the other, to Joel. Naturally, they were both a perfect fit! A dear friend, Dick Bock, filmed the event and that moment has been preserved for me to relive each time I see the film.

After the house opening, we returned to Swami's house where He complimented my mother on the beauty of the garland. He asked that she place it in the refrigerator in a back room to preserve it. A garland, after its use, is usually placed on statues or pictures of gods and then discarded; we wondered why Swami wanted to keep it. What we thought might be a gesture of appreciation turned out to be foreknowledge of an event to follow.

The following day, Swami performed the remarriage of Elsie and Walter Cowan. In India, after a couple is in their sixties and their children are grown, worldly obligations are finished thus leaving them free to dedicate themselves to spiritual matters. At this time, it is a custom to perform a remarriage symbolizing the beginning of a new life together with God. We had advised Elsie to bring Swami a special garland for the ceremony but she felt, as many people do, that such formalities are not necessary as Swami does not care about such things.

Slowly, I was learning to follow Swami's teachings on dharma (right action). Right results can only be obtained by right actions. Understanding the right action at the correct time is a most difficult and subtle matter and one spends a lifetime studying and applying righteousness. Observing Swami, who is dharma (righteousness) personified at all times, was a great lesson in learning how our lives should be conducted.

When the Cowans arrived, Swami greeted Elsie with a surprise. He presented her with an elegant gold dress and matching shawl that He had ordered to be made especially for her. Elsie was not able to wear saris because at a certain age it is difficult to learn to drape them and adapt oneself to moving about comfortably wrapped in six yards of material. Swami asked my mother to take Elsie to another room and help put on the new gown. When Elsie was dressed, Swami came to give the final inspection; the dress was a perfect fit, but Swami was not satisfied with the manner in which the shawl was draped at the shoulders. With quick, agile hands and the know-how of a skilled fashion designer, He expertly rearranged the shawl and tied it in a most elegant style.

"Where is the garland?" Swami asked the Cowans, looking around for it before performing the ceremony. "We did not bring one, " the Cowans answered apologetically. For a few moments Swami feigned a sad, forlorn expression, as though the ceremony could not be continued without it. We waited in suspense for Swami to find a solution. He then turned to Mother, as if He had just thought of the idea on the spur of the moment, and asked that she fetch the garland placed in the refrigerator the preceding day.

The very moving and elevating ceremony continued, during which Swami explained the spiritual significance of remarriage. Next, the Cowans garlanded Swami with Mother's beautiful rose creation and towards the end Swami materialized for them two ruby rings.

Elsie was very much at ease and spontaneous with Swami, so much so that sometimes she addressed Him as "Honey." But on this occasion, when she addressed Him in this manner, and perhaps because there were quite a few people present who might have ideas of imitating her, Swami took the opportunity to teach the proper and respectful way of addressing Him. He replied, "My name is Sri Sathya Sai Baba." In Elsie's case, she was not being disrespectful but natural and spontaneous. I have seen instances where people attempted to be discourteous but Swami never allowed such behavior to continue. If He was not able to correct them verbally, He would leave the room and that person was never invited back .

Joel, who loved jokes, would often crack up with great gusto at Swami's humor. Joel had worked as a stand-up comic and had a large repertoire of stories and jokes he wanted to share. He made a few attempts to entertain at this time but because he was not sensitive to correct timing, the effort flagged. Swami, always on the alert, discouraged Joel by ignoring him and Joel quickly developed a more respectful attitude. He eventually realized that with Swami, he could not play games or compete by showing off. We were there to observe and learn.

Swami's unmatched, delicate and refined sense of humor was a soothing balm that heals body and soul. When He made us laugh, a surge of pure joy filled our being, refreshed us and we felt completely revitalized.

THE CRYSTAL JAPAMALA

*Do not come to me with your hands full of
trash for how can I fill them with grace when
they are already full. Come with empty hands
and carry away My treasure, My love.*

Sathya Sai Baba

One of the most memorable interviews I wit-
nessed in the front room at that time was Ravi Shankar's first
interview with Swami. This well-known Indian musician
was giving a concert in Bangalore at the time. He came to
see Swami accompanied by one of his musicians. Ravi sat
quietly gazing at Swami but his eyes revealed the intensity
of devotion and reverence he felt for this noble presence.
Into this current of love, we were all enveloped and felt the
invisible thread of oneness that binds us all together as
flowers in a garland. With tears in his eyes, Ravi listened
while Swami revealed incidents in his life, his feelings and
thoughts. Swami pointed out to Ravi that his music was not
ordinary; it was divinely inspired.

When Swami asked Ravi what he desired, Ravi
replied humbly with love, reverence and slight surprise as

though he had already received everything in the world by being in Swami's presence: "Only your darshan." Swami, apparently pleased with the answer, waved His hand and materialized instantly a beautiful diamond ring which He placed on Ravi's finger. He told Ravi to wear it when he played the sitar. After the interview, all went outside and pictures were taken of Ravi together with the rest of us. In the following years, Swami invited Ravi Shankar to perform several times in the Poornachandra Auditorium in Prasanthi Nilayam on the occasion of the celebration of Swami's birthdays.

Initial interviews are particularly inspiring to witness because of the extraordinary impact felt by the person seeing Swami for the first time. On those occasions, we have an opportunity to share another's joy so intensely that we experience unity with them, as well as the rest of mankind. Slowly the Brotherhood of Man dawns on us.

On another occasion, Swami again took us to the riverbed. But unfortunately this time, a crowd of uninvited guests managed to slip in and the atmosphere was not as special and intimate as before. Dick Bock had been invited and Swami permitted him to film as He materialized statues of Indian gods and goddesses and withdrew them from beneath the sand. Swami also materialized the most beautiful crystal japamala (prayer beads) I had ever seen. Myriad colors blazed forth from the crystal beads which glistened as though alive in the light of the moon. I felt an irresistible attraction and desire to possess the japamala and secretly hoped He would give it to me.

A few days earlier, Swami had noticed a sandalwood japamala that I was wearing. He said He would give me a better one as the one I was wearing was not very good. With the aspiration that this crystal japamala was perhaps meant to replace my old one, I held my breath in anticipation when He passed the japamala around for everyone to see. But quickly my hopes and heart sank when He gave it to another lady. I consoled myself thinking that this heavenly japamala was much too beautiful for me and after all, why wish for more material objects when they cause nothing but unhappiness anyway. I had no idea then that the reward for giving up a desire was often its fulfillment at a later time.

We had been with Swami for four months and the time to return to the United States was quickly approaching. Joel liked our routine there because Swami was paying so much attention to him and this boosted his ego. Also, Swami frequently introduced Joel to other guests as the "world's greatest director," which was Joel's dream. He had worked for eight years as assistant director to Orson Welles in England. After he came to the United States, he sold many scripts and acted on television but he was never again able to become a successful director: the pursuit he most desired.

In Swami's residence, Joel met many interesting people from all parts of the world and he delighted in talking with them. Each day with Swami was a new and exciting adventure but a very different type of excitement from what he had been accustomed. It replaced entirely the old diversions of night clubs and parties and he felt happy and content with this life. After his business failed, Joel had nothing left in the West but three houses in Los Angeles. Now that Swami had given us a home, he was thinking of selling the Stateside houses and living permanently in India.

During our last interview with Swami before returning to California, we asked His permission to come live in India. Swami immediately agreed, but told Joel to keep one of the houses for his mother and sell the other two. And then, quite suddenly, Swami waved His hand and materialized a glass japamala. I stretched out my hand to receive it, certain it was for me. Instead, Swami handed it to Joel. I thought it was strange for Swami to give Joel a japamala that he did not desire or even know how to use. Perhaps He was renewing a desire I thought I had given up for the crystal japamala.

In the car, while leaving Brindavan, I grumbled that it was not fair of Swami to offer to give me a japamala and then not keep His promise and yet, a part of me was relieved as I did not actually like the glass one which Joel received; my mind was set on the crystal beads.

Mother, who was returning to the States with us, wanted very much to buy me a crystal japamala and when we reached our hotel in Bombay, she insisted that we take a taxi and search for one. We spent the rest of the day roaming through specialty stores and temples but could not find crystal beads, only those made of glass, wood or stone.

Then the unexpected happened! Our plane made an unscheduled stop in Tel Aviv because of a bomb threat. Consequently, we had to deplane and could not leave until the following day. As soon as we arrived at the hotel, which the airline had provided for us, we were approached by a gentleman who very politely insisted we should not miss this opportunity to see Jerusalem. We were very tired but his gentle, persuasive manner convinced us to go.

In the very first shop we entered, inside the walls of the old city, we saw two crystal japamalas exactly like the one Swami had materialized. They were the only two in the store. The japamalas had the correct number of beads which is extraordinary because neither the Christian rosaries nor Muslim prayer beads have the same number of beads. The price for each was exactly nine dollars (nine is a divine number). Could it be by chance that all these coincidences took place in the Holy City of Jerusalem? At that moment, I remembered what one great scientist once told me, "When one coincidence after another takes place, it can no longer be labeled a coincidence."

We departed Tel Aviv the next day for Los Angeles. Once there, we sold the houses, put our household furnishings in storage and returned to my beloved India for what was to be an unforgettable three-year extended sojourn with Swami.

Bhagavan
Sri Sathya Sai Baba

PRINCAVAN
WHITEFIELD
PHONE NO. 33

DATE:

Dear Rajagopal! Accept my Blessings and Love
All are happy days to a man of true knowledge
Happiness is an internal conscious experience
which comes as the effect of the extinction of a
mental or physical desire. The lesser the desires,
the greater is the happiness. So that perfect happiness consists in the destruction or ~~satis~~
Satisfaction of all desires in the Absolute being
Greatness is really independent and does not
depend upon externals. it is the sense of perfection or the consciousness of the achievement of
the highest end of life that is called greatness.
Fame among many people is not called greatness
in its strictest sense. The answer is more a
question of definition, and the definition depends
on the view-point, culture and experience of each
man.
goodness is not false or impossible, but is the
one factor which gives real value of life. Life
without goodness is not real life. but only a scene
of the destructive dance of the evil forces which
shall drown the individual in grief. Goodness is
the way to true happiness. In the ultimate
analysis there is no separate entity as goodness
it obtains only in the relative plane. where duality
is transcended no question of pairs of opposites
arises. Raju GroD is always with you in you Be happy
— Baba —

Raja! I am sending little prasad (vibhudi)
for your health. your health is not good
Be healthy and happy

With Love
Baba

HOME, THE RESTING PLACE

For the bird in mid-ocean flying over the deep dark blue waters, the only resting place is the mast of a ship that sails across it, from one shore to another. In the same way, the Lord is the only refuge for man, who is swept by storms over a restless sea of troubles.

Sathya Sai Baba

When we returned to India, Swami invited us to resume the same routine and activities as before. Again, we had the full, daily schedule, the only difference being that we did not have to go back and forth to the hotel as we had moved into our house. Now we were able to start the day with Swami's darshan which He gave from the balcony of His bedroom every morning at six.

After breakfast, we would sit in the front room of Swami's house and wait for Him to come downstairs. He would then chat with us and sometimes look through the newspaper (waste paper as He called it) and make comments on the daily news. His many comments would include a spiritual or ethical teaching, so for us it was a digest paper. At these sessions we learned much of what Swami approved or disapproved and what he expected or wanted from a devotee. Daily, He would go through stacks of personal letters received through the mail or collected by Him at darshan. Often, He would comment on the trials and tribulations of others giving us great insight into proper behavior and right action.

Around nine in the morning, He would go outside to give darshan to the hundreds of people that gathered daily. When He brought the visitors to the front room, we were delighted to observe the interplay, so different and novel each time between Swami and each person. He usually gave the person —seeing Him for the first time— a memento, so we witnessed hundreds of materializations and creations, each uniquely different and divinely splendid giving unsurpassed joy to the receiver and to us.

Twice a day, Swami would offer us tiffin (a snack) and sometimes invited us to join Him for lunch in the downstairs dining room. Later, the dining room was moved upstairs and became more private as fewer people were invited to join Him. Other times, we might go home for lunch, rest until about four in the afternoon and then gather again in the main room. Since Swami gave darshan in the afternoon also, the morning routine would be repeated with the new visitors that He chose.

In the evening, the college boys (Swami had just started a boys' college in Whitefield) would gather in the main room of His residence to sing bhajans. At this time, Swami would often play small cymbals. Often, on these occasions, a complete transformation would come over His face as He kept perfect rhythm and His delicate hands struck the cymbals with graceful gestures. His face took on a most youthful appearance, aglow with a soft, blue hue. We were so captivated by His enchanting beauty during those moments that we sat transfixed, and all the while, the sounds of the bhajans faded in the distance. After bhajans, either Swami, one of the college boys or a college professor would give a talk. Swami would usually retire around eight in the evening.

With such a full schedule, I did not have time to attend to household duties. Also, Christina could not be expected to sit in the front room every day for so many hours at a stretch so I hired Stella (the ayah I had found on the previous trip) and her husband, George, to cook, shop, clean and care for Christina.

I wish I had kept a journal during those years as each day with Swami would make an inspiring chapter of a book; every word and action of His was a learning experience. The greatest miracles are not so much those seen by the eyes, but those that unfold and transform the inner self. We are unaware of the process until we look back, years later, and marvel at the strange and very different person we used to be before we knew Swami. He brings about our transformation slowly but steadily while patiently holding our hand and guiding us in His chosen direction. We hasten to reach the summit and often find the path burdensome and steep. We then need to remember patience and permit Swami to guide and direct us, placing full trust and confidence in Him.

Those experiences and incidents that occurred during that three-years period are imprinted indelibly in my mind. They will never be forgotten because they were the most important years of my life. Actually, they are the only years that can be counted because until I started making the journey home towards God, I was standing still and going nowhere.

****

At times, when Swami would sort through His vast correspondence, He would sit humming to Himself and sometimes hold an envelope in His hand for a moment as though mentally reading the contents. At other times, He would open and read a letter. Occasionally He would pore over a letter for a long time; it was almost as if He were savoring every word. We would sit quietly, with our eyes transfixed on His ethereal beauty and our ears enchanted by the soft melodious humming which filled the room with a celestial ambiance.

The mood would change when a visitor who doubted was present. Swami would then reach for an envelope from the stack of mail and announce from whom it came or its contents. He repeated the process several times until, perhaps, the visitor was convinced. Once, with a mischievous smile, He picked up an envelope and tore it in half, discarded one half and delicately reached into the other half from which He pulled out a neatly folded little note. This action greatly amazed the visitor who must have thought, by his look of surprise, that Swami had mistakenly torn the letter.

Some mornings, we would sit through long sessions of questions and answers with Dr. Hislop (who later was appointed President of the Sathya Sai Baba Council of America by Swami). For hours, Swami would patiently clarify each and every question asked, until Jack was thoroughly satisfied. After the session, Jack would return to his room and write down every precious word. Later, with Swami's permission, he published the questions and answers in his books, *Conversations* and *My Baba and I*.

While the group was small, Professor Gokak would translate from Telugu into English excerpts from a book that Swami had written. It was a book that Swami said would not be published for a long time as the world was not ready for it. It was about the secrets of the creation of the world, mysteries of the planets and solar system, the decline of humanity and other fascinating subjects. We were all absorbed and eager for the next day's unveiling of mysteries. Sadly, the reading stopped as soon as more visitors arrived. The book, to this day, has not been published.

Some of the visitors were fascinating people and we learned a great deal and admired many of them. One such person was the Maharajah of Kutch. He would come occasionally to see Swami and visit his daughter, Princess Nanda who was a regular guest at Swami's residence. She is the dear lady who trained us from the very beginning to wear our saris properly, how to recognize the unspoken rules and the proper etiquette of Indian customs. She also would interpret Swami's remarks and jokes made in Indian languages for which we were most grateful. Westerners rarely have the opportunity to hear the most fascinating things Swami says because Indians are often reluctant to translate.

We noticed that the Maharajah had a huge, thick, silver bracelet around his ankle and we asked him if it was not uncomfortable when sitting cross-legged. His reply was most touching and devotional. He explained that he had the bracelet put on his ankle to remind him always of God. Every few years it would become loose and he would have it tightened, so that it would always be uncomfortable and that way he would never forget God.

****

Swami's reality cannot be grasped by the mind. I have found that when interacting with Him, a veil of illusion clouds my vision by the very effort of having to use the mind to verbalize and identify Him with His form. He has assumed a human form because we would not be able to relate to another form. What would we do before a burning bush or say to a light brighter than a million suns? When we are with Him, if we are able to still the mind and reach the very core of our being —beyond name and form— we can experience the impersonal aspect of Swami that is pure love. That, we are soon thrilled to discover, is also our own true nature.

The most elevating, beautiful time I ever spent with Swami was in total silence. One morning, Irene (a devotee from Hawaii and guest in our house) and I went to Swami's house quite early. By chance, on this particular day, no one had yet arrived and Swami was sitting alone in His chair. We took our usual positions directly in front of the chair and sat quietly facing Him. Not one word was spoken. Swami was playing with a rose and occasionally He glanced over at us. For about twenty timeless minutes, it was as though only the three of us existed in the entire universe. Such a deep feeling of peace and love filled our being that we felt as though our bodies had disintegrated as we melted into an ocean of bliss.

****

Swami would divide His time between Brindavan and the ashram at Prasanthi Nilayam, and we were allowed to follow only with His permission and invitation. We quickly learned that His permission to both follow or leave was essential.

Once, after having been in Prasanthi Nilayam a long period of time, Joel longed for more comfort and good food and decided to go to Bangalore for a few days. Swami was occupied with a building project and Joel felt we would not be missed. We traveled only a few miles out of the ashram before we had a flat tire and no spare as a replacement. In those days, cars did not travel back and forth as frequently as today. We sat under the scorching sun, in the middle of nowhere, for the entire day before help came to return us to the ashram. That evening, Swami chided Joel for leaving without permission and told him the flat tire was a small reproof.

I cannot say which place I preferred, Prasanthi Nilayam or Brindavan: selfishly, probably Brindavan because the entire day was spent in Swami's presence. But Prasanthi Nilayam is an enchanted place like no other, and at times I felt it to be a heaven on earth with which no fabled paradise could compare. Especially in the earlier years, when the crowds were so small compared with today, it had a much warmer and more intimate atmosphere as Swami was able to interact and move more freely among His devotees.

The daily schedule also was quite different at Prasanthi Nilayam. At six every morning, He would stand on the balcony of the mandir (temple) and give the most powerful and beautiful darshan of the day; so uplifting was the impact of its beauty, that the effect would last until He appeared the following morning. One would float through the day with just the memory of that divine darshan.

Every evening, our day would end with a smile as we watched little Sai Gita (Swami's elephant was just a baby then) carry a garland in her trunk and then gently place it about Swami's head. His devoted elephant would then bow reverently to Him. Swami would tenderly stroke her and speak sweet words while feeding Sai Gita her favorite fruits from a basket.

I used to go to the river and watch Sai Gita bathe. The Chitravati river was then a broad and deep river with a strong current. At that time, I wished that I could play and splash like Sai Gita in that sacred river, but in India ladies bathe wearing saris. Swimming with six yards of material is very unpleasant. When I heard that if you bathe in a sacred river like the Ganges, all your sins are washed away, I devised a method. I had a tailor make me a long, simple dress with pleats in the front (so it looked like a sari) but consisted of only a few yards of material. Then I was able to swim comfortably in the Chitravati and the wash-and-wear material would dry by the time I arrived back at the ashram which was a walking distance of only a few minutes.

Even though I considered the Chitravati a holy river, even holier than the Ganges since it was flowing through the village of Swami's birth and He often swam in it in His youth, I never felt it washed away my sins. Perhaps because it was a borrowed belief or simply because I found sins to be endless; as soon as you wash one away, you unintentionally or invariably commit another.

****

I was often filled with a longing to serve Swami and there were times when that desire was fulfilled with great satisfaction: such as when He asked me to serve tiffin to Brindavan guests. But, I had not experienced the supreme joy of serving Him personally. I used to observe Raja Reddy (an attendant who at that time was often with Swami) running at full speed anytime Swami asked for anything; then, he would return just as quickly and wait eagerly for further orders. How I longed also to be able to run and perform Swami's command; I felt there could be no greater satisfaction. But, that was not possible because Swami did not have lady attendants. My desire remained a dream, until one beautiful day which will always be dear to me.

On this particular evening, Swami came to visit us quite unexpectedly; Raja Reddy was with Him. It was dinner time. A big pot of rice and vegetables was on the stove. Knowing it was customary to offer a small amount to Swami on such occasion, I served Him a portion. In India it is the custom to eat with one's right hand and Swami politely took a small amount with His hand and ate it. Immediately, Raja Reddy observed that Swami's hand needed to be cleaned and started to give Him a handkerchief. At that moment, I shouted mentally but not audibly, "Oh no! Don't take the handkerchief. This is my big chance!" In that instant, Swami glanced over at me, raised His hand indicating refusal of Raja's handkerchief, then looked back at me. With that cue, I ran at full speed to another room to get a handkerchief. Swami patiently waited until I returned to clean His hand and give me the most precious gift of serving Him.

****

Often, when newcomers are not seen by Swami, I have heard them complain that He sees only those who are wealthy or important. I know from personal experience that this is not true. I could find numerous stories to tell but usually the following story is enough to silence them.

A friend of ours was the late wealthy and prominent Baron Albert Rothschild. When he visited us in Ojai, California, we told him about Swami and he became so interested that he went to India to learn firsthand. When he was in Brindavan, Swami was informed that the Baron was outside among the crowd at darshan but Swami would not see him.

Instead, when a large group of Nepalese, too poor to afford any type of transportation, walked all the way from Nepal to have Swami's darshan, His heart melted at their devotion. He immediately invited the group to His house and served all of them lunch personally. On that occasion we, too, were permitted to serve the Nepalese who assembled under the veranda because the dining room could not accommodate their great number. Swami did the heavy work of scooping food from the buckets. And all the while He would stoop low over each and every person's plate and talk with and bless each one. Many, too moved by Swami's display of love to start eating, kept their teary eyes fixed on Him and their hands joined in reverence. The servants of the Lord found the Lord Himself serving them.

Swami, later, highly praised the Nepalese and brought to our attention how these people were filled with the spirit of sacrifice and true devotion. I felt so small; I wanted to crawl away and hide. Compared with them, I had done nothing to deserve sitting at His feet and listening to

His spiritual discourses day after day. I felt ashamed and unworthy, but most of all I felt as though I had taken this great opportunity with Swami for granted. This feeling was reinforced when on one occasion Swami said to me: "You don't know how lucky you are!" That day, I understood my ignorance and resolved to try harder to be a better if only a very small person.

****

There were periods when, for months at a time, Swami would give spiritual discourses every evening in the main room at Brindavan. These spiritually uplifting talks uncovered precious gems of truth and provided much guidance and instruction. It is most unfortunate and lamentable that, at that time, there was no one present to record His words.

One evening, when Swami was giving one of these fascinating talks, a huge beetle—with dangling, spiny legs— flew in through an open window. I was terrified of the creature. It buzzed noisily and was as big as a hand. I had visions of it getting entrapped in my hair, squirming on my scalp trying to get free only to become more entangled. How would I get it loose? I would need scissors which I did not have to cut it loose. All the people were sitting in rapt attention listening to Swami; I could not move, much less leave. If it flew in my hair, I would have to sit still and endure it. I followed the beetle's every move with that unbearable thought, and could no longer pay attention to what Swami was saying. Before the beetle flew in, I was totally concentrated and absorbed in Swami's particularly enlightening discourse.

Swami was standing on the other side of the room—on the men's side—and not even facing my direction. Suddenly, He stopped talking, walked over to the beetle and scooped it up with His hand. He looked down at me and while holding the harmless beetle in His hand, gave me the sweetest, protective and all-knowing, fatherly smile as He tossed it out the window. He then walked back and resumed the discourse. How much more than any human father does He guard and protect us from our real and imaginary fears?

Sai Baba with author and Joel in Brindavan.

THE MERCIFUL LORD

*Joy comes to man not through the shape of
things, but through the relationship established. Not any child, but her own child makes
the mother happy. If one establishes that kin-
ship with everything in the universe, what an
overpowering joy could be experienced. Only
those who have felt it can understand.*

Sathya Sai Baba

Swami's love and compassion are so deep that if
we, each, could develop but a small amount of it towards
our fellow man, we would instantly be in the "Golden Age."

Being an animal lover, I had adopted every stray,
hungry dog in Brindavan that managed to sneak through
the compound gate. They would take turns coming to our
house at different times to be fed. They knew, if they did
not leave quickly, they would be driven out by guards at the
gate. A few of my eat-and-run regulars were: Coffee, which
had mange; Juliet with her bleeding, open sores; Blackie that
had asthma; and Rama, which was the healthiest. Then
there were two others, Sita and Romeo that were much

braver and took the chance of staying around longer. Later, because of Swami's generosity they became permanent residents in the compound.

Sita was a big, black female with expressive brown eyes and a sweet disposition. I have seen her wagging her tail even while being beaten. Romeo, poor fellow, had been run over by a car and left partially paralyzed. To compensate, his front legs had become so strong that they were powerful enough to drag the rest of his limp body and he was able to move very quickly. I loved these two dogs especially and gave them the best possible food and care.

One morning, upon arriving at Swami's house, I was told that Swami had called the veterinarian. He was scheduled to arrive any moment for the purpose of putting Romeo and Sita to sleep. The night before, a calf that died of rabies had been buried. Sita and Romeo had dug up parts of the dead animal and consumed it. Since it was almost certain that the dogs would be infected and be a great danger to people, there was nothing to do but destroy them. I understood there was no alternative.

This news was too unbearable for me. Since I could not contain my anguish, I left Swami's house to find the dogs. I cried profusely as I said goodbye to Sita and Romeo for the last time. Then, gathering all my strength, composed myself so I could return to Swami's house without showing my childish outburst of uncontrolled emotion. Arriving back at Swami's, I saw Him pointing out to the veterinarian the infected dogs. I had to run back in the house as I was unable to face the inevitable.

Swami went directly out to give darshan and the veterinarian left. The other guests came back to sit in the house waiting for Swami's return. Again, I went outside. There were Romeo and Sita wagging their tails at me! What happened? Swami had spoken to the veterinarian, but none of the foreigners understood what was said. Then, Mrs. Ratanlal appeared. Very calmly and matter-of-factly, she spoke the most beautiful words I ever could have dreamt of hearing: "Swami materialized vibhuti for the dogs and fed it to them. He said He had to save them or you would cry too much!"

Sai Baba with His elephant Sai Gita.

SAI GITA'S DESIRE FOR THE LORD

Be assured that the Lord has come to save the world from calamity. Your duty is to keep calm, and pray for the happiness and prosperity of all. You cannot be happy when the rest of mankind is unhappy.

Sathya Sai Baba

When Swami spent months at a time in Brindavan, Sai Gita His elephant would walk from Puttaparthi and stay in the Brindavan compound with her trainer. She would spend most of the day under a tree below Swami's balcony where all of us gathered for morning darshan. Swami would pay a lot of attention to her, daily petting her and feeding Sai Gita her favorite fruits. She is a very gentle and loving creature, but as a precaution, her trainer would always chain her foot loosely to a tree.

For several days, Swami had been very busy and had not been able to see Gita. And, just as many devotees do, she snapped under the strain of being ignored too long. She broke the chain and, loudly trumpeting, started galloping wildly all over the compound. Her trainer ran after her and tried to control her, but ended up under her belly, miraculously unhurt as she ran past him waving her trunk madly in all directions and trumpeting thunderously.

Joel and I ran to grab Christina who was playing under the trees nearby. When Joel saw Gita's trainer still lying on the ground and no one able to stop her, he decided to do it. I yelled at him not to go and that he could get killed. A crazed elephant is not a creature to be tackled, even by an expert. But he paid no attention and ran, yelling, "Sai Ram," and positioned himself in front of the charging elephant with his arms outstretched.

I closed my eyes, unable to look at what I expected to be his death. A second later I opened them. There stood Joel affectionately patting Gita on the trunk and telling her what a good girl she was! She had come to her senses and to a screeching halt. Was it Gita's sense or had Swami heard Joel's courageous plea when he shouted, "Sai Ram" and called on Him for help?

That afternoon, Gita had big tears rolling down from her eyes as Swami consoled her by lovingly stroking her trunk and feeding her a basket full of her favorite fruits.

THE DIVINE LIGHT

*The moment you realize that you are not the
body, then at that very moment all the attach-
ments and delusions will disappear.*

Sathya Sai Baba

My mother, being psychically sensitive since
birth, is often able to see things in other dimensions of
existence—invisible to the eye—but nevertheless, just as
real. Often, when looking at Swami, she would see His
forehead smeared with vibhuti and kumkum (red powder)
and a halo around His head or body.

Once, as we were returning from darshan, she told
me how particularly beautiful the light around Swami's
body was that morning. Her description of its beauty
created an intense desire in me to see this light. I was feeling
sorry for myself for being so dense and unable to see anything beyond the range of the ordinary.

The next morning, I went to darshan feeling a little
gloomy. As I looked up at Swami, I saw an intensely bright,
electric-blue light that radiated brilliantly about a foot and

a half from His entire body. It was magnificent! But I could not believe what I was seeing. I felt it must be my imagination, perhaps created by the intense desire I felt the previous day. So, I blinked my eyes to see if it would go away if I did not accept it. It did not. When I looked up again, the blue light was even more intense in color and radiated out farther. It seemed to be pulsating. When Swami moved, He took the blue light with Him and left a white light that outlined His body where it had stood before.

It took me several moments to accept this vision. As I let go of doubts, I started experiencing a wonderful feeling of an elevation of consciousness beyond space and time, to the ever present NOW. It was a state of BEING where no divisions exist and thought is absent. I finally understood, or better, experienced the saying: "Be still and know that I AM."

Quite often after that experience Swami (with only a glance) would elevate my consciousness to this blissful state of BEING. That is, undoubtedly, the greatest miracle and divine grace one can receive in order to develop faith. If faith is not based on experience, it has no foundation and can at any moment crumble.

Swami Himself, after He has built up the faith in a devotee, will inevitably test that faith. He will see if He can shake our faith and cause it to crumble. For our sakes, He holds a mirror up to us so that we may see ourselves. My test was also to come, though not for many years; for now, I was overflowing with the love He poured into my previously empty cup.

GINGER WAITS FOR SWAMI

Your heart should be filled with compassion towards all living beings. You should fill the suffering hearts with prema (love). You should radiate thoughts that can generate ananda (blissful peace).

Sathya Sai Baba

In 1972, Swami planned a month-long summer course on spirituality and Indian culture to be held at Brindavan. Three hundred students from various colleges throughout India, as well as seniors from Swami's college and guests attended the summer course. The students were housed and fed in Brindavan for the entire month. Swami personally supervised every detail of the daily schedule and the intense, spiritually oriented curriculum. The many-faceted program centered around the Indian heritage of moral and spiritual wisdom, and study of the lives and messages of mystics and saints of all creeds and countries. Talks were given by scholars, pundits, writers, judges, professors, artists and poets from all parts of India and abroad. Swami ended each evening with His divine discourse. Ultimately these month-long summer courses were to be held each year through 1979. Swami's discourses were later published as a series of books titled *Summer Showers in Brindavan*.

The first summer course took place under a large tent that extended from Swami's residence to within a few feet of our house. One morning, as Swami was walking around inspecting the area, He stopped at our house where the end of the tent was being assembled. "Would you like to attend the summer course in comfort, under a fan?" He asked us sweetly. "Oh, yes Swami. That would be wonderful," we replied without thinking; we were not sure what He meant but it sounded good. Then Swami explained that if He left the back of the tent open, we could sit on the beds that were right against the window and have a perfect view of the speaker. He said a platform would be constructed at the front and we would be able to see above the rows of chairs. We were delighted! Sitting for thirty days on metal chairs, eight hours a day (in the humid, sweltering summer heat of India) would have been quite an austerity. He also informed us that Mr. and Mrs. Murphet were arriving soon and He wanted to put them in our spare room.

Howard and Iris Murphet arrived shortly before the summer course began from Adyar, the Theosophical Society headquarters in Madras. Howard had spent some time there doing research for two books he wrote about the founders of the Theosophical Society. He later was to write three books about Sai Baba: *Sai Baba Avatar, Sai Baba Man of Miracles* and *Sai Baba Invitation to Glory*.

We did have a most comfortable arrangement during the summer course. We were able to listen to all the talks (including Howard's) in the company of the Murphets on the soft mattresses and under the fan with plenty of food and cool drinks. But for me, it turned out to be an emotionally painful period and I was grateful that Swami interceded to lessen the physical burden.

For the first few nights, Howard and Iris were unable to sleep because my dog Sita was in season and had chosen to sleep under their window. There, of course, all the male dogs in the neighborhood gathered to compete for her attention. I had no choice but to take Sita to the veterinarian and have her spayed. I was reluctant and worried because I knew how sparingly anesthetics were used on animals.

A few months before, Sita had given birth to a litter of puppies and we were able to find homes for all which is an accomplishment in India. I kept one, a real delight, which we named Ginger. Swami admired our sweet, chubby Ginger and asked that she be brought upstairs to His balcony where He played with her like a little child. Everyone admired her and told me she was a most blessed and fortunate little puppy. During the summer course, because of the crowd, I kept her inside our enclosed front porch.

One afternoon, Swami materialized vibhuti for Joel and told him it was for his stomach. Joel was a bit surprised because, at that point, he felt fine; his stomach was not in the least upset. That evening, he went with a friend to a village nearby to eat dinner and the trouble Swami had foreseen started. Joel woke up in the middle of the night as sick as the proverbial dog. I should say, as sick as the dog. Ginger also started vomiting and the two of them had terrible cases of diarrhea and vomiting that continued through the long night, accompanied by loud moans and groans.

Joel recuperated in a few days but Ginger did not. The veterinarian had no idea what she had or how to cure her. She did not have the strength to stand and had lost all self-control. The servants were constantly cleaning the front porch and the poor Murphets had to put up with the disagreeable situation every time they used the porch, the only access to their room.

For days I debated what to do. I could not bear to watch Ginger's suffering and yet did not believe I had the right to take a life I did not create. I felt only God could do that. Ginger was semiconscious now and constantly whimpered and moaned. Every day I thought would be her last, but the days dragged on. Finally, I could not withstand her suffering any longer and decided, right or wrong, to end it. The veterinarian gave her what should have been a fatal injection but when I brought her home, she was still faintly breathing. I laid her on the porch, put vibhuti on her forehead and said a last prayer for her.

A resident doctor and animal lover who had been advising and consoling me through the whole ordeal, came to the house while I was performing the last rites. Upon seeing Ginger still alive, the doctor told me: "We don't know the level of consciousness in this little puppy who has been so lucky as to be blessed by Swami. Now, she is so fortunate as to be able to attend the summer course. I suspect on some level she is taking it all in and has no intention of dying until the summer course ends." A dog listening to the summer course? I certainly loved animals, but I could not accept such a level of understanding from them.

I returned to the veterinarian suspecting he skimped on the quantity; he was baffled. With genuine concern, he assured me that he had given Ginger a portion large enough to have killed a much larger animal. I believed him. By now, I was more aware of the limitations of "free will." We think we are free to act and undoubtedly we should act to the best of our abilities as though we are; however, there are many times when we need to let go and accept the decree of a higher will without resistance.

I understood I could not give her another injection, so I suffered it out with my little Ginger and gave her plenty of vibhuti. After Swami's discourse on the very last day of the summer course, Ginger died. Had she actually, on some higher level, understood and willed against all odds to stay alive to the last day? Was it a lesson for me to let go and let God? Quite truly, it was much more than I could grasp, but it certainly was astonishing that she took her last breath immediately after Swami's final discourse as my doctor friend predicted.

Sai Baba seated in front of the forest-tour bus in the Bandipur Forest.

THE GHOST

*May the pure and the righteous rejoice! The
wicked and the false, the cowardly and cruel
may also rejoice, for He in His mercy will lead
them back onto the holy path. If I close the
door against the sinful, the fallen and the
renegade, where else can they go?*

Sathya Sai Baba

Howard and Iris Murphet were still with us when
Swami invited all five of us to go to Ooty with Him. Ooty
is a mountain resort about eight hours by car from Bangalore. Joel, along with a few college boys, drove the jeep (a
devotee had given the jeep to Swami and He let us use it for
three years) and Christina and I went in a car with the ladies.

Swami had sent several hundred rupees to Joel to pay
for the gasoline for the jeep. When we stopped to have tiffin,
the men and Swami had tea while the ladies walked around.
Howard told me that during tea, Joel had tried to return the
gas money to Swami only to be severely scolded. Swami
admonished him, explaining that a child does not seek to
repay the mother. The mother does everything out of love,

97

not compensation. Offering to return the money indicated he did not understand his relationship with Swami. Joel was so ashamed, he never mentioned it to me.

About half way to Ooty in the Bandipur Forest, we boarded a forest-tour bus. Swami sat in the front and pointed out to us many wild animals, including a herd of wild elephants roaming carefree in the Bandipur Game Sanctuary. Late in the evening we arrived in Ooty. The house where we stayed was later purchased by Swami and converted into a school. It was an old, two-story English-style villa.

After a delicious dinner with Swami prepared by the volunteers in His organization, we retired for the night. Our room was next to the Murphets and directly beneath Swami's room. In the middle of the night while I was asleep —but on another conscious level, and aware of being next to my physical body —I sensed the presence of an evil being just outside the door. I knew its intention was to harm me; its very nature was dark, cruel and diabolic. A tremendous fear gripped me and forced me to wake up.

I have always been sensitive to, and able to feel, the presence and vibrations of spirits and I knew this one was an unusually strong and demonic being. I awoke Joel but he did not sense anything except a cold, chilling breeze that swept into the room in spite of the windows being closed. I refused to go back to sleep knowing that the creature could reach me only in the sleep state. Joel, realizing my agitated condition, searched around and fortunately found a kerosene lantern. In spite of there now being light in the room, I could not sleep more than a few minutes at a time; I feared the ghost might return regardless of the light .

The following day, I could hardly wait to tell the Murphets the house was haunted. Howard laughed at the whole idea, but later when he was talking to Swami, he related to Him my fears of the place. "Yes," Swami confirmed, "there were some very bad people in this house. After some time of singing the bhajans, they will go."

In the evening the people gathered outside the house for darshan, were invited inside for evening bhajans. Swami's behavior, too, was most unusual during bhajans. He sat in His chair with a strange look on His face. He would look up in the air with a frown and repeatedly shake His head as if disapproving of something that was invisible to the rest of us. Later that evening, I advised the Murphets to sleep with their lantern lit just in case one night of bhajans was not enough to drive the ghosts away. Howard was still skeptical and did not light the lantern.

In the morning, poor Howard could hardly talk, his throat was hurting so much. He managed to tell—with a hoarse voice and horrified expression—about a huge, black, evil mass that jumped on his chest while he was sleeping and tried to strangle him. He awoke still aware of trying to fight the creature's grip around his throat. Where the creature touched the chest and neck, he continued to have intense pain. For the remaining seven days spent in Ooty, we all slept with lanterns. There were bhajans every evening at which Swami persisted in his gazing into the air, frowning and disapproving of something mysterious.

During this period, Swami gave a most inspiring talk to hundreds of soldiers at a nearby army base and the entire week was filled with activities during the day, and quiet dinners with Swami in the evening. One day, Swami took us for a picnic to one of the highest lookout points in the beautiful mountains surrounding Ooty. Being in the midst of nature and the uplifting setting of the high mountains with Swami, was truly breathtaking. Here, one felt transported to the presence of the great God Shiva (a mighty Hindu god) whose legendary abode is in the Himalayas.

It was so bitterly cold that I do not know how Swami managed with His thin robe and bare feet. Yes, I do know, but it still made me cold to look at Him. The rest of us caught a terrible chill from the biting cold. It's difficult to always remember that Swami is not like us. Just the previous evening, when I looked at His bare feet on the cold floor, I forgot He was above the bodily senses and offered Swami a pair of warm booties that I had brought. He laughed, and reminded me that He does not need such things, as even when He traveled to the mountains in the north of India, He walked barefoot in the snow.

Swami's divinity was usually the subject for argument between Joel and me. One evening we argued back and forth about whether Swami needed to sleep or not. I was certain He did not sleep. What would happen to the world if He slept? Joel insisted His body was no different from ours. In the morning, as Swami came downstairs, the first thing He said to me with a twinkle in His eye was: "Swami never sleeps!"

The incident with the ghost and the fact that it was able to come so close to Swami, disturbed me. As soon as we returned to Brindavan, I started telling the old-timers (devotees who had been around Swami since His youth) what had happened, asking them for explanations. They laughed at me for being so naive, and expecting only good people or angels to surround Swami. When bad people approached Him, what did I expect Swami to do? Send them away? If He sent them away, who would help those who needed Him the most?

When a theft had been committed in the ashram, Swami's comment had been: "The thief also broke a coconut to me." (This is a religious ceremony where one waves and breaks a coconut to one's chosen form of God.) Swami said all were His children. He felt equal love for the good and the bad. He did not come to help only those who were already good, or to prevent people from engaging in wrong actions. That would make Him a dictator, exercising power to control people. Swami does not control us; this would prevent our learning the laws of the universe. If we do not learn, we can never grow and evolve to the point of choosing to love God.

Swami said He can turn earth into sky and sky into earth, but He does not have the power to move man's heart one inch towards God. Choosing to love God, I believe, is the one thing He has given us complete freedom to do. By giving every one of us His love, with no distinction between the deserving or undeserving, He is giving us the only thing that has the power to make us change willingly.

When I thought of Swami as a mother, with both her good and naughty children gathered about her, it was easy to understand the episode with the ghost. But, at the beginning, I asked many questions and tried to clear away as many misconceptions as possible. I did this because I did not want to build faith on a weak foundation, only to fall away later because of unresolved doubts and misunderstandings.

How often I have I seen devotees leave Swami because of what they perceived to be an injustice due to their lack of understanding and inquiry. As far as the mind can reason and clarify such matters, it is best to apply it, provided we recognize the right time to discard the mind and trust the heart. I noticed that those who appear to be the most ardent and enthusiastic believers were often the first to fall away from Swami, perhaps because they did not build their faith on a solid foundation.

Sai Baba with author, Joel and Christina in Ooty.

DOES SWAMI NEED AN INTERPRETER?

There is only one language, the language of the heart.

Sathya Sai Baba

Whenever Swami had an interpreter, I noticed invariably that He would correct the interpreter, thus indicating that He did not require his services. Therefore, it was only a formality when He did choose to have one.

On one occasion, I had an excellent opportunity to see how quickly ignorance and delusion overcome us. This occurred when Swami called me one day to interpret for an Italian couple from Sicily who did not speak English. I felt so happy and proud to be of assistance to Swami and interpreted into Italian, in which I am fluent, carefully and precisely everything He told me in English. While I was speaking in Italian, Swami suddenly stopped me and corrected my translation saying I had misinterpreted a word.

Instantly it hit me. Who did I think I was, that I could assist Swami, who knew Italian far better than I ever could? It was out of His great love and kindness that He was assisting me, by creating a need for an interpreter, and thus giving me the opportunity to be in His much desired and uplifting presence.

My mother had a similar experiences. Once she was corrected by Swami while interpreting in German. Another time, Swami asked her to interpret a spiritual discourse (a much more difficult task than an interview) that Swami gave to the first large Italian group which came to the ashram.

Dr. Bhagavantham translated Swami's Telugu into English for Mother, who in turn translated into Italian. While Mother was speaking to the group in Italian, Swami stopped her and explained directly to her in English the area she had misunderstood.

Swami's use of an interpreter will remain a lila (play) to be enjoyed by the language of the heart that needs no interpretation.

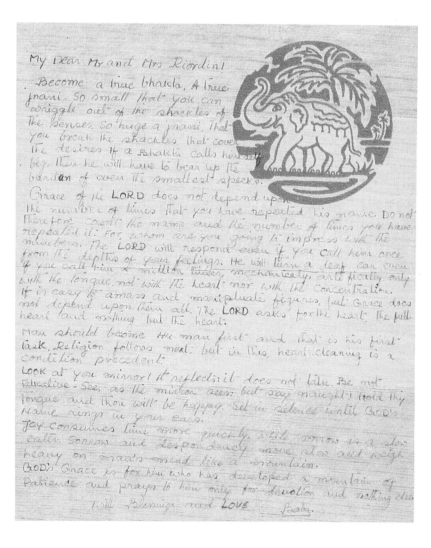

My Dear Mr and Mrs Riordin!
. Become a true bhakta. A true jnani so small that you can wriggle out of the shackles of the senses so huge a jnani that you break the shackles that cover the desires. If a bhakta calls himself big then he will have to bear up the burden of even the smallest specks.
Grace of the LORD does not depend upon the number of times that you have repeated his name. Do not therefore count the name and the number of times you have repeated it: For whom are you going to impress with the numbers. The LORD will respond even if you call him once from the depths of your feelings. He will turn a deaf ear even if you call him a million times, mechanically, artificially only with the tongue, not with the heart nor with the concentration. It is easy to amass and manipulate figures, but Grace does not depend upon them all. The LORD asks for the heart, the full heart and nothing but the heart.
Man should become the man first and that is his first task. Religion follows next; but in this heart-cleaning is a condition precedent.
Look at your mirror! It reflects: it does not talk. Be not talkative - See, as the mirror sees: but say naught. Hold thy tongue and thou will be happy. Sit in silence until GOD's Name rings in your ears.
Joy consumes time more quickly, while sorrow is a slow ... Sorrow and despondency move slow and weigh heavy on man's mind like a mountain.
GOD's Grace is for him who has developed a mountain of Patience and prays to him only for devotion and nothing else.
Hail Blessings and LOVE   Baba.

Due to the passage of time (this letter was written 20 years ago,) the ink has faded. A printed version is shown on the following page for easier reading.

My dear Mr. and Mrs. Riordin!

Become a true bhakta, a true jnani. So small that you can wriggle out of the shackles of the senses. So huge a jnani that you break the shackles that cover the desires. If a bhakta calls himself big, then he will have to bear up the burden of even the smallest specks.

Grace of the LORD does not depend upon the number of times that you have repeated his name. Do not therefore count the name and the number of times you have repeated it. For whom are you going to impress with the numbers. The LORD will respond even if you call him once from the depths of your feelings. He will turn a deaf ear even if you call him a million times, mechanically, artificially only with the tongue not with the heart nor with the concentration. It is easy to amass and manipulate figures, but grace does not depend upon them all. The LORD asks for the heart, the full heart and nothing but the heart.

Look at your mirror. It reflects: it does not talk. Be not talkative. See as the mirror sees: but say naught! Hold thy tongue and thou wilt be happy. Sit in silence until GOD's name rings in your ears.

Joy consumes time more quickly, while sorrow is a slow eater. Sorrow and despondency move slow and weigh heavy on a man's mind like a mountain.

GOD's grace is for him who has developed a mountain of patience and prays to him only for devotion and nothing else.

With Blessings and LOVE,

Baba

JOEL

*At first, name and form are essential. That is
the reason why Avatars come, so that God can
be loved, adored, worshiped, listened to and
followed, and finally realized as Nameless and
Formless.*

Sathya Sai Baba

Joel had a most unusual relationship with Swami,
unlike that of any devotee I have ever seen. He understood
very little of spiritual matters. Without such background, it
was difficult for him to come to any reasonable conclusion,
especially about the Avatar. He understood only what he
saw. And what he saw was a "Superman" capable of the
most extraordinary feats he had ever witnessed, but an
inkling of Swami's true reality Joel never had. Nor did it
matter to him if Swami was divine, human or from the
planet Mars. He loved Swami with all his heart, and often
referred to Him as "my best friend."

He was not in awe of Swami, as most devotees are,
but protective and caring of his "friend." His attitude was
so different, that it often amused, and probably disturbed

some devotees who observed his interaction with Swami. Often when Swami materialized or distributed sweets, Joel would comment, "But Swami, you haven't had any, please have some first." Swami would explain that He does not take sweets, but Joel would not accept "no" for an answer. Having a sweet tooth himself, Joel wanted to share the pleasure with his "friend." Swami would sometimes give in (He generally never eats sweets) and take a very small piece, just to make Joel happy but, once, when distributing chocolates, Swami stood His ground and refused to take even a small piece.

On one occasion, Swami came to our house with Raja Reddy, and Joel explained to Him the construction plans that we had made for the inside of the kitchen. Swami offered a particular suggestion to which Joel replied with the exclamation: "Swami, that's a brilliant idea!" Raja Reddy and I could not contain our laughter and surprise at such a naive statement. Joel made many such statements that could be considered naive or refreshingly simple and childlike.

One morning, Swami came downstairs from His bedroom and sat in His chair. As He started rubbing His knees, He said: "There is so much pain." We all looked at each other alarmed at such a statement but unable to ask why, as Swami got up and walked out for darshan. Joel immediately followed Swami with a grave expression of concern. We ladies were not allowed to follow when He gave darshan, so we stayed behind whispering speculations and anxiously awaiting His return.

Upon His return, we noticed that He was having difficulty walking. Instead of staying downstairs until lunch as was His custom, we saw Him heading for the stairs that led to His bedroom. He started to climb, but could not. Joel quickly rushed over to Swami (when none of the other men would dare), lifted Him in his arms and carried Him upstairs. A few of the men, who were allowed upstairs, followed, while we ladies tearfully rushed outside. In a state of shock and grief, we gathered under Swami's balcony in silence and prayer, hoping someone would give us news of His condition.

When Joel finally came down, he walked towards the ladies. In doing this, he broke the rule that men and women should not speak or stand together publicly (unless they are related). Pathetically and with tears in his eyes, Joel stated that Swami was paralyzed from the waist down.

The week that followed was filled with tension and anguish. If Joel had not had access to Swami's room and brought us news, it would have been a nightmare. Swami's house was deserted and we were closed up in ours. None dared go outside the compound for fear of being questioned by those seeking information. We did not want to give fuel to more rumors and speculation in this time of sorrow.

When Joel told us of Swami's great pain and described how the doctor stuck pins in Swami's delicate legs to test for numbness, we begged him to ask Swami to distribute His pain among us. We wanted so much to help and felt powerless to do anything for the One we loved most. Joel imitated Swami's gesture of pressing the index finger tightly against the thumb, and said Swami stated, "Even distributed among you, none could endure even this much of the pain."

Our servants told us that one of the many rumors circulating was that Swami had been poisoned, but the explanation that Swami gave was never made public. Swami said that some very powerful yogis were testing Him to determine if He really was the Avatar. They were sending Him, what best could be compared to currents of very high voltage, enough to kill a human being instantly. He could not return the energy force to them because they would die; thus, He accepted it, adding that ultimately these yogis —by this act of His— would become His devotees.

After one week, Swami miraculously threw off the paralysis as He had always done with any illness that beset Him. Overnight, He was once again His usual self, acting as if nothing had happened. How wonderfully happy we felt seeing Him well again. And Joel, feeling unusually chirpy during early-morning darshan, found himself beneath Swami's balcony. Joel saw Swami there and instead of assuming the folded-hand posture of reverence, gave Swami a brisk military salute. Swami laughed and saluted back.

****

Swami put Joel's theatrical talents to good use when he placed him in charge of directing a play performed by the college boys. Joel's nerves were tested on this occasion when Swami went out of town just before the first performance of the play. Swami had added another chore for Joel: He asked Joel to paint His house (any color Joel chose) and have it ready upon His return.

It was pandemonium! Joel was running in all directions. Between rehearsals with the boys, he drove to town for supplies, bought paint, rigged ladders and designed stage sets. When the deadline for painting the house could not be met (except by working through the night), he enlisted the aid of the college boys. At dawn, he was the only one left; one by one, the boys had dropped away from exhaustion.

When Swami returned, He was pleased with the color of the house but not with Joel's keeping the boys up to paint as they were too tired to study. Swami always gave priority to school work. Joel had much goodwill but had lacked foresight and discrimination. Swami can be a strict disciplinarian, but we learned quickly that goodwill alone is not sufficient, unless it is carefully balanced by discrimination to determine whether the end justifies the means.

****

The morning following an interview Joel and I had with Swami, Joel was still in a very serious mood. During the interview, Joel had asked Swami some rather profound questions. "Swami, if you are God and I am God, is there a supreme God?" "Oh, yes," Swami replied. "What is God?" Joel asked. Swami gave him a most unusual reply, "When the positive and the negative meet, without resistance, that current is God."

Thus it was that Joel sat contemplating Swami's words from the day before. And it was in this frame of mind that he told me he needed to be alone, to try and understand it all. He left to climb the isolated hills of Puttaparthi outside the ashram. When he returned, he was beaming with happiness. He told me he had just been through the greatest religious experience of his life while sitting on a rock in the hills. He had heard the voice of God! A voice had spoken to him and answered every question he asked. He felt certain it was the voice of God, because the doubts were gone and all the questions were answered. Joel concluded that these things could come to pass only through the loving authority of one who knows and can convey the gift of understanding.

Joel was greatly inspired by this experience and composed a beautiful poem which later was published in "Sanathana Sarathi" (the monthly magazine distributed by the ashram). When he gave the poem to Professor Kasturi, he asked to remain anonymous because he could not take credit for "His loving Father's" inspirational words to him.

Dear loved one, you ask,
"How will you know when I am near you?"
When on a sultry night
everything is hot and still,
The first cool breeze brushes your cheeks
Think of me.
When the pangs of hunger are satisfied
And loneliness is pierced by happiness
Think of me.
When your mouth is parched
And you can hardly speak,
The first sip of cool water
I am soothing you
Think of me.
When I sprinkle your face with cold rain
and wash the earth, the dry brown leaves,
The first smell of clear rain
I am cleansing you
Think of me.
When pain dissolves
And tears disappear
Think of me.
When steadfast eyes are horrified
By the cruelties of life,
The first glance of the silent setting sun
I am comforting you

Think of me.
Then you ask "How will you know when you are
near me?"
When the burning sun
Has scorched you and the earth,
The sand and dust fill your eyes
Not a sliver of shade about
And you love me.
When loneliness is accompanied by
hunger and not one can be satisfied
And you love me.
When your lips are cracked
Your tongue feels like clay
Your throat seals up
There is not water about
Not even a mirage in sight
And you love me.
When pain becomes unbearable, you smile
And you love me.
When I take from you
Your most cherished possession,
on the first loss of sight
darkness envelops you
And you love me.

For everything that you see, hear, smell, taste or
touch belongs to me. So how can you give to me
what I already own but your love? And that, I gave
to you before time began as your soul's possession.
When you return it to me then I will know you are
truly mine and I will dissolve your sorrow and hap-
piness into me. That one being me, I will place you
in bliss forever. For I love and think of you con-
stantly.
From your most loving Father

His loving Father's words were made tangible, one morning, in the form of a letter. Swami was sitting on the outside steps of His bedroom writing as he often did. In those days, He was writing the *Vahini* series (a series of books on His teachings) in longhand, which Professor Kasturi later typed and translated. We were watching Him from below. Swami finished a letter and carefully folded it; He inserted the letter into an addressed envelope, and stood up. We all moved closer, as that was an indication that He might want to talk to one of us or that He would be going downstairs. We were always like buffaloes (as He used to call us), ready to stampede in herd fashion, following Him anywhere. Swami called out, "Rowdy," (another nickname for Joel) while motioning for Joel to come closer. As he did, Swami threw the envelope down to him.

I was so excited and curious to see the letter but could not go near Joel as all the college boys crowded around him. Joel was not sure if it was for him alone or if he should let the boys see it. Swami solved his dilemma by telling Joel to read it. I noticed immediately, when I saw the letter, that Swami had misspelled our last name. It was addressed, "Mr. and Mrs. Riordin." It should have been spelled RiorDAN, but Swami wrote RiorDIN. I could not understand why until much later, when I learned that DIN means, "to argue."

BHAGAWAN SRI SATHYA SAI BABA

BRINDAVAN WHITEFIELD PHONE : 33

PRASANTHINILAYAM P.O. ANANTHAPUR DT. PHONE : 30

Raja! Accept my Love and Blessings
I received your sweet letter. How are you Raja?
Be happy. don't worry. SAI is always
with you.

Renunciation is the power of battling against
evil forces and holding the mind in check
It is Truth and Truth alone. that is one's
real friend, relative, self, (Atma) Abide
by. Truth, tread the path of righteousness
and not an hair of your body will ever
be injured.

You are not to be perfect; you are that
already. Nature is like that screen which is
hiding the reality beyond. Every good thought
that you think or act upon is simply tearing
the veil as it were, and the purity,
the infinity the GOD behind manifests itself
more and more

Raja! once you Come, must come to summer
Class ate may (20, 5-78,) to 20, 6, 78. (with Love)
—— Baba ——

Dear Raja! How are you? How is
your health? don't worry! Swami is
always with you. in you around you.
Be happy. with Love and
Blessings
—— Baba

Above: Sai Baba with author, Christina and Mother in Brindavan.
Below: With author, Christina and Joel on the occasion of the Hislop's house opening in Brindavan.

CHRISTINA

I require from each of you no other gift, no more valuable offering than the heart I have endowed you with. Give me that heart, as pure as when I gave it to you, full of the nectar of love I filled it with.

Sathya Sai Baba

Christina adjusted beautifully to life in the ashram. Often I would take her with me to Swami's house where she was capable of sitting for eight hours or more without complaining. Swami invited her to attend many public functions, and gave her guest badges to events where most children were not allowed. He demanded a great deal from such a little girl, but His reward for her perfect discipline was enormous. The love and attention He showered upon her almost daily brought much joy to our hearts.

Once, when Swami came to our house, He sat down on the couch with Christina and read her nursery rhymes from one of her books. They both laughed like children as Swami joked about the Ba Ba in "Ba Ba Black Sheep." Another time, He was giving saris to the ladies and Christina looked sad and disappointed; immediately He went upstairs to His room and returned with an adorable little Western-style dress for her.

He would encourage her, telling her what a good girl she was, and tease her when she sucked her thumb saying she would end up looking like Sai Gita (His elephant) with enormous teeth that protruded awkwardly. When I had a miniature sari made for her, He teased her, saying she looked like an airline hostess —the sari was blue with white checks— because stewardesses on domestic Indian flights were similarly attired. Swami made us all laugh when He imitated the way Christina walked: like Charlie Chaplin, He said. It was a perfect description of how she would clown around.

Swami had great fun with one of Christina's dolls. On one of His visits, Swami asked Christina to show Him her dolls. One doll had a string coming from its side. Each time the string was pulled, the doll would say a different short sentence in a child's voice. Swami was delightful as He laughed, full of surprise each time He heard the doll speak. He kept pulling the string to see what it would say next.

At that time, Swami was preparing the boys to per-form in a play called "Shankaracharya." Rupak, one of the most talented, was playing the leading role of Shakaracharya (a well-known Indian saint). Every evening, we were invited to watch the rehearsals that took place in Swami's downstairs dining room. With great love and patience Swami corrected and improved each boy's perfor-mance; over and over they rehearsed until each scene was perfect.

During a dress rehearsal, one of the boys playing a mother holding a baby, was not holding his arms properly because he was lacking the make-believe baby. Swami thought of using Christina's doll and sent her to get it. He then took the doll and cradled it gently in His arms, showing the boys how a baby should be held. When everyone was thoroughly engrossed in admiring this most tender scene of Mother Sai and the baby, Swami pulled the string. Out came this squeaky little voice that said: "I want to go night-night." The boys roared with laughter. At that time, a talking doll was a great novelty in India. Swami repeated the same prank, amusing everyone backstage when the play was later performed at Prasanthi Nilayam in the Poornachandra Auditorium.

Swami's nephew and wife lived during those years in the downstairs portion of Swami's house. They had two children: Vidyullatha, a girl Christina's age, and Sai Kiran, a boy a few years younger. They were the only other children in the compound. Despite the language barrier, the children got along beautifully and developed a deep friendship while sharing many adventures together.

One day, when Christina was about four and a half years old, Swami was outside watching her play in the cow shed. He turned to me and said, "Too much play." I understood that He was hinting it was time for her to go to school and learn, instead of wasting time playing. But where to enroll her? After some investigation I found there were two schools in nearby Whitefield: The Glass Factory School and St. Joseph's Convent. I enrolled her first at the Glass Factory, as it was a preschool and later at St. Joseph's, where she was joined by her friend, Vidyullatha. The two girls would walk together every day accompanied by Stella, the ayah.

Before I could enroll her, an important issue had to be resolved between Joel and me. Joel wanted her to have immunizations and I did not. I was strongly against immunizations and had never given her any since birth. The strongest medicine she ever had was Tylenol, because I used medicine only as a last resort. Although Joel did not agree with my views about medicine, until now he had let me have my way. He felt that she had been protected against the outside world by living in the compound, but now that she would be coming in contact with many children it was too risky not to have her immunized. We debated and argued back and forth for days, and when we could not compromise, we decided to ask Swami to resolve the dilemma.

When asking Swami a question, one's state of mind and the words selected are most important. As Swami says, He reflects and mirrors us. If our desire is not for truth, but merely for what we want to hear, He may simply reflect our desire in His answer. Many people ask Swami if they can do this or that, and His answer is, "Yes, yes." Whereas, if the question had been, SHOULD I do this or that —together with a willingness to hear the truth—Swami's answer might very possibly have been, "No."

Before asking Swami about the immunizations, I had to do some work on myself. I had to be willing to do what was best for Christina; that is, put aside my stróng opposition to medicine and be willing to carry out whatever Swami suggested. I also had to resist the temptation of phrasing the question in such a way as to point a finger at Joel, such as: "He wants Christina to have shots." Implying in this instance that I did not, in which case Swami might take my side, but only because He reflected my desire.

When I was inwardly ready to do His will instead of mine, I asked Swami, "Should Christina have immunization shots for school?" "What shots?" Swami asked, but answered before I could speak with a chuckle, "She has already been immunized by playing in the dirt and drinking the dirty water from the well."

After some months Christina became very ill; her temperature was over 104 degrees F. for days and Tylenol could not bring it down. I called a doctor from Whitefield, but he was unable to help. It was beginning to look very serious. I usually tried not to disturb Swami and asked for His assistance only after I had exhausted all other resources. Finally, fatigued and desperate, and feeling her condition was reaching a critical stage, I carried Christina to Swami's house and asked for His help. He looked down at her most lovingly and said, "Don't worry, it's just malaria." He materialized vibhuti, poured some in her mouth and smeared the remainder on her forehead. "Tomorrow the temperature will go, she will be all right," He assured me. I placed her little body at His feet with gratitude.

The next day, Christina's temperature subsided and she started recuperating. She never had another occurrence of malaria (as is often the case) and Joel had to take back his, "I told you she had to get shots," because she did not get the illness from lack of immunizations, but from a mosquito.

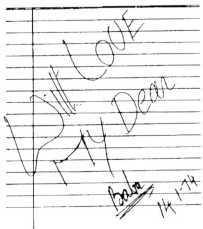

Sai Baba holding Christina in the courtyard of his home in Brindavan.
A loving message written in Christina's notebook by Sai Baba.

THE DUES HAVE TO BE
PAID

Whenever I appear to be angry, remember, it is only love in another form. For, I have not even an atom of anger in Me.

Sathya Sai Baba

Mother and Christina accompanied me on the second trip to Ooty with Swami. Joel, with Swami's permission, had returned to California a few months previously to monitor his gold investments. The market was fluctuating erratically, and he felt he needed to be in a position to act quickly to prevent a great loss. Quite frankly, I was happy about his absence as we never had a day without tension and arguments. My mother, Christina and I were alone in the house and, together, we always had a wonderful time. Now we were going to Ooty with Swami for ten days, what heaven!

The cars did not leave in the usual caravan style (all following Swami's car) as that might have alerted passers-by on the road, and word about Swami's travel plans would quickly spread. Instead, Swami gave us a rendezvous place just outside of Bangalore from which the cars could safely proceed together. We all left in different directions and at different times.

Mrs. Patel (the tomato-soup lady) and Dr. Bhatnagar (the one who helped me with Ginger) were in our car as we drove quickly to the rendezvous place and waited for Swami and the others to arrive. We waited and waited but no other cars appeared. A debate followed as we tried to decide how to proceed. I was influenced by my great eagerness to get to Ooty, which I loved . Also, I felt Swami must have gone ahead as the delay was too long. My mother and Mrs. Patel both knew that the unwritten rule was to always remain behind Swami, so it would not be proper to go on ahead of Him to Ooty. But, since the delay was so great, we thought it prudent to go a bit farther to see if He actually was in front of us. Consequently, we resumed the journey hoping to catch up with Him and the rest of the cars. The driver was unfamiliar with the road but, as I remembered the way very clearly, I was able to guide him.

Needless to say, we never encountered the rest of the contingent and continued on to Ooty which we reached very late that evening. We noticed immediately, by the number of anxious volunteers outside the house, that Swami had not arrived. We felt mortified at our lack of judgment and sat quietly in the room (the one I had occupied on the previous trip) and waited. After about four hours, Swami and the others arrived. Swami came straight to our room and in a very strong and severe tone said: "Where were you? Do you know that I waited four hours for you? I sent the boys up and down the roads looking for you." He did not even pause to give us a chance to answer, but went on scolding.

Swami is so powerful in feigning anger that we felt as small as ants, and wished we could have disappeared into the ground. Of course, at the moment, we did not think or react as though His anger was not real.

Once, when Swami had scolded another lady, I was so shaken that I asked Swami if He actually had been angry. He laughed and answered that He never gets angry, for if He should, He would burn everything to ashes. Many times I have seen Him give someone a terrible scolding and then, just as suddenly, break into the sweetest smile possible. In a split second, Swami can transform, as even the greatest actor is not able to do, to any range of expression and emotion.

As soon as Swami left the room, all the ladies pounced on us, full of indignation and anger that we had dared to let their beloved Lord wait for no less than four hours. Who did we think we were? they asked. We could not have felt more depressed and remorseful due to their feelings and Swami's reaction towards us. It was in this forlorn state that we closed ourselves in our room, prayed to be forgiven and spent a most miserable night.

The following morning, without any of the ladies seeing Him, Swami came to our room and was His sweet, usual Self. In fact, He greeted us as though nothing had happened. We touched His feet with gratitude and followed Him to the dining room for breakfast.

For the entire ten days that we were in Ooty, we did not join the ladies but spontaneously followed our intuition. We would take walks on the lovely mountain paths while the other ladies were all gathered together in a room, waiting to find out where they were expected to go next or what the daily schedule would be. (When traveling with Swami, or staying with Him, His guests are never given much advance notice and the day is spent watching, listening and always being ready to move quickly.) Since the ladies were still angry with us and not speaking, we did not join them.

By Swami's grace (it had to be grace because our intuition could not have been so consistently sharp), we did not miss a single event or spiritual discourse. Always, and just at the right time, we would end our walk and return to the house, and find an important event about to take place.

Even on New Year's Day, and quite early in the morning, we felt led to the bhajan room where we found Swami standing alone. We touched His feet; He gave us sweets and we spent precious, quiet moments with Him. In those days also, it was very rare for Swami to be alone. He was continually surrounded by people. When traveling, He always took a few of the college boys along and, of course, there were the ever-present crowds of devotees.

Swami's room was directly over ours, and several of the college boys who shared the room with Him told us later that they could hear every word we said. We felt very bad upon learning this, as we must have kept the boys awake and disturbed Swami. Mother and I often laughed and joked in Italian, and we must have made quite a racket.

We also learned later, from one of the men who was in the car with Swami, that when the cars had been separated on the way to Ooty, Swami had sent boys looking for us pretending He did not know where we were; but, He assured the man there was nothing to worry about. Swami told him that Mrs. Rajagopal's daughter (me) was at that moment directing the driver of the car to the house in Ooty. His dramas are often baffling.

On one occasion, Swami took us to a scenic lookout site on one of the many high peaks surrounding Ooty. At one point during the picnic, we noticed that two boys lifted Swami in their arms and placed Him inside His car where He sat alone for sometime. All of the ladies gathered with folded hands around the car and stared at Swami. We felt strongly that He had isolated Himself because something was wrong. It saddened me that often, we devotees, are so insensitive and inconsiderate of Swami's privacy. We stood at some distance away from the car and waited. Finally, and without leaving the car, Swami gave orders to the boys to drive Him home. We found out later that, in fact, Swami had not been well and was in pain during the picnic and while sitting in the car.

Even though He is divine, He resides in a human body and there are instances when, for reasons He does not always explain, His body takes on pain. Often, He takes upon Himself the pain of His devotees which would be too unbearable for them to endure; at other times, He accepts the pain for reasons that we will probably never know. It has occurred to me many times that we devotees are totally unaware, and sometimes inconsiderate, of His needs. We usually think only of ourselves, and ask from Him constant acknowledgement of our existence, yet are totally insensitive to His.

Also, there may be instances when, due to a high fever or foot injury, Swami will withdraw when devotees try to touch His feet. And just as often, His followers will become more persistent and aggressive. Some may go so far as to hurl themselves and grab His delicate feet so forcibly as to throw Him off balance. Others, sulking, might retreat because they believe themselves to be at fault or that they have conducted themselves improperly. Very few, if any, just accept what He does without self-centered speculation.

On our return trip to Brindavan from Ooty, we had car trouble just past Mysore and had to wait exactly four hours to have it repaired. Our karma caught up with us quickly. Even with Swami's forgiveness the dues had to be paid!

THE HEAVENLY
BHAGAVATA

*Is there anything sweeter than all things
sweet, more auspicious than all auspicious
things, holier than all holy objects, verily, it is
the name of the Lord or the Lord Himself.*

Sathya Sai Baba

After we returned from Ooty, I decided to take full
advantage of Joel's absence and read the *Srimad Bhagavata*.
I had been reading all the Indian scriptures I could find, and
learned that the *Bhagavata* was written by the sage Vyasa
specifically to instill devotion to God in the reader. The only
version of the *Bhagavata* that could be found in book stores
was condensed because the original was too lengthy and
tedious for most people.

This sacred book cannot be read just like any other
book. The sage gave instructions that it be read completely
within seven days while partaking only of fruit and milk,
and sleeping on a bed of special kusa grass; there were other

provisions also. The *Bhagavata* was an experience. I was determined to find it and live it.

I had searched through every bookstore in Bangalore before being directed to the Vedanta Bookstore where, I was told, the entire version was indeed available. The book had just been published recently by a non-profit organization as a service to humanity. The original Sanskrit appeared in the book, and directly beneath each passage was an accurate English translation made by learned scholars and pundits. It was available in two volumes and comprised 1700 pages. The salesperson stated that the bookstore had ordered several copies which were expected any day. "Any day," in India, can mean any month I learned after four months and many trips to the bookstore.

Only the strong desire to read the *Bhagavata* gave me the courage to attempt driving the jeep in India. The roads there are better obstacle courses than any military unit could hope to devise. Motorists drive on the left side of the road which is shared with motorcycles, bicycles, rickshaws, pedestrians, monkeys, dogs, horses, cows and numerous donkeys that hop slowly with front legs tied together so they cannot run away. It took all my powers of concentration and many "Sai Rams," but the effort was well rewarded. You can imagine my great surprise when, on my first driving attempt, I arrived at the bookstore at the very same moment that a bullock cart pulled up carrying my precious *Bhagavata*.

Avidly, I followed the book's instructions as closely as possible. Many instructions, of course, simply could not be adhered to, like sleeping on kusa grass. Kusa grass is a special kind of sacred grass that I could not find; I made other minor adjustments also.

The sage's promise of instilling devotion was more than fulfilled. What I experienced during those seven days was a continuous state of bliss, on an elevated plane of consciousness that I can only describe as heaven-like. Not for a moment did I come down from that blissful state. The inner communication with Swami was phenomenal. No words were necessary; I experienced oneness and unity between Him and me. No sooner would I have the desire to touch His feet, than He would come and stand before me, offering His beloved feet to satisfy my yearning to express devotion. I would be contemplating the love between mother and child, and He would tenderly call me "Amma" (mother). Throughout the whole seven-day period and for several weeks following, He confirmed the unity I experienced in so many ways that, even when the experience of elevated consciousness ended, I could never doubt or question its reality.

I have found in myself and in other devotees that we often ask Swami for proof of His omniscience, and after He gives it, we say it must have been a coincidence. So we ask for another proof, and then still another. There comes a time when, no matter what He does, our minds cannot be satisfied and will find some cause to waver. That is the time when we have to discard that part of our limited mind that doubts, and replace it with a heart full of faith, trust and commitment; there is no other way. The mind will always protect and take the side of the ego which is the enemy of the spiritual aspirant because it knows that God is its destruction.

SWAMI'S LILAS

*To earn the good will of the Master, there is
one recipe; obey His orders without murmur.
Grace is showered on all who obey instructions and follow orders.*

Sathya Sai Baba

After a few blissful and very peaceful months,
Swami asked me: "How is Ravana?" He would often jokingly refer to Joel as Ravana, the ten-headed demon of the
Indian classic, *Ramayana.* "I don't know Swami, I haven't
heard when he is coming back," I replied. "Oh, he is not
coming back until 1982," Swami said, grinning broadly.

One never knows exactly what Swami means or how
to interpret His words. They could be symbolic or factual.
An event could happen right away or in the future. His
words could require deep meditation, inquiry or introspection, or they could simply be taken verbatim. Many of the
things He has told me I have not understood until years
later. Since correctly interpreting His words is so difficult,
I have always taken Him literally at the moment and then
waited. If what He said did not happen, I tried introspection

and meditation. If I still could not understand, then, it was only a matter of time (and my waiting patiently) until the meaning became clear.

Why is it that Swami does not speak clearly and tell us everything precisely? No teacher does. Christ and the prophets spoke in parables. At different stages of maturity in our lives, the same words will often have different meanings and, most importantly, we pay no attention when we are told the fire is hot; we have to touch it. The greatest and most permanent teacher is self-discovery.

In this case, I believed what He said about Joel's return in 1982, but did not wait long enough to take action. Joel and I had wanted to divorce for some time, and of course we had asked Swami's permission. No answer came from Swami and I mistakenly interpreted His silence and assurance that He would talk later on the subject, to mean that this would be the beginning of my freedom. I calculated that since 1982 was about eight years away, Joel probably would remain in the States, send divorce papers from there, and I would be able to live in India peacefully ever after.

So, I had reached this point in my thinking, when one day my mother and I decided to go to Bangalore to have a good lunch and celebrate. Before leaving, I went through Joel's closet and gave all his shirts and pants to our servant, George. Of course, George and his wife, Stella, were delighted with all the presents they were getting and the news that Joel was not returning.

That evening, we were all on the front porch enjoying the evening breeze before retiring, when suddenly, the porch door opened. There stood Joel! "Didn't you get my telegrams?" he said with a jolly face. No one said a word.

We stared, waiting to see if he would go away; perhaps he was just an apparition. "Isn't anyone going to say 'hello' to me?" Joel said, staring back. No one moved or spoke except Christina, who ran up to her father and hugged him. My mother quietly slipped away to her room. George, embarrassed because he was wearing Joel's clothes, took Stella into the kitchen; I followed Joel into the bedroom. I could not find an explanation for our strange behavior, except to tell Joel precisely what Swami had said. Joel, naturally, was very upset and perplexed by Swami's statement.

In the morning, he went to talk to Swami, determined to get an explanation. Swami was very sweet and loving and completely diverted Joel's attention from the subject by suggesting that the two of them go for a ride in the jeep. I do not know what was said on their trip, but when they returned Joel was pacified; he forgot all about the incident. Later that day, Swami, Colonel Jogarao and my mother left for Prasanthi Nilayam and I was left alone with my "apparition" for a week to recuperate. The shock I received was enough to give me a high fever.

For years, I thought about the meaning of this incident. I talked about it and asked old devotees for their opinions. For many inexplicable occurrences, the Indians will often comment, "Oh, it's just one of Swami's lilas." Lila, means "divine play." Many Hindus, especially those on the path of bhakti (devotion), feel that the universe is God's playground, created by Him for His amusement. He plays with us without any rhyme or reason and we have to let go and learn to enjoy the game; flow with life without resistance. Learn to accept and put our questioning mind aside. Yet, Swami says, "I don't do anything without a reason." So, how can we learn if we do not think about the meaning of

His words and make changes in our lives? I think the key is surrender. So long as we have not surrendered, but take on the role of the "doer," we are responsible and are obligated to assume responsibility for our lives, acting as best we can under the guidance of our guru. When we reach that point when we can surrender the "doer" portion of ourselves, our responsibility has ended. So —in a "doer" state of consciousness—to dismiss happenings prematurely as lilas, is a lazy way to avoid doing our homework. I don't think it is possible to understand the entire concept of lilas unless we are in a divine state of consciousness.

I waited eight years to discover that this particular lila did have a reason; it was a reminder of Swami's omniscience. In 1982, Joel had a stroke and became partially paralyzed. In a hospital in Los Angeles, he not only felt Swami's hand on his heart, but actually saw it and touched it; after which, he completely recovered from the paralysis. He telephoned me from the hospital and told me about it, adding that he felt Swami was calling him to Prasanthi Nilayam. He did not want to go to India alone, and asked my mother (by this time we had divorced and I was remarried and living in Ojai) to accompany him, but she was unable. His doctors strongly advised him against leaving the hospital and they recommended immediate heart bypass surgery. He had already had three heart attacks. My mother, stepfather and I spent hours on the phone with Joel, trying to convince him against the surgery. We reminded him of many people, including a lady he knew well, who had sought Swami's intercession under the same conditions (against the advice of doctors), and had returned completely healed. Pressed by his doctors, and frightened with speculations of what might happen if they did not operate immediately, he yielded to their recommendations. Joel never regained consciousness following the surgery.

As Swami predicted, the Rainbow Man came back to his permanent home in 1982.

Offer all bitterness in the sacred Fire and emerge grand, great and godly.

Sathya Sai Baba

Sai Baba blessing Mother. Story page 141. Below: Sai Baba in His Brindavan home with a statue of Lord Ganesha. Story page 143.

MANTRAS AND PRAYERS

Prayer is the very breath of religion; for it brings man and God together and with every sigh, nearer and nearer.

Sathya Sai Baba

A very moving episode, which proved beyond a doubt the tremendous power and efficacy of mantras, was the story of the birth and consequence of the repetition of the Sai Gayatri.

The Sai Gayatri was given in a dream to a lady who later wrote it down. During darshan, this lady was sitting next to Mother; she handed the paper to Mother and asked her opinion. Before my mother had a chance to look at the paper, Swami was standing in front of her, calling her for an interview. With paper in hand, she went for the interview. Swami, upon seeing the paper, took it, glanced at the writing and exclaimed: "This is the Sai Gayatri. Say it; it's very good." After the interview my mother repeated the Sai Gayatri to a few people. Very quickly, knowledge of it spread throughout the ashram.

Sometime later, my mother again made reservations to be in India for Swami's birthday. At the same time, she received a cable from my grandmother in Switzerland saying she was very ill, and to please come soon. She knew that two trips would involve too much time spent away from Raja, her husband, so, when she asked his permission to go, she told him she would cancel her trip to India and go only to Switzerland. She considered helping her mother a pressing duty that had to be fulfilled.

In November, as Swami's birthday grew closer, she regretted having told my stepfather that she would cancel the India trip because she was feeling a tremendous longing to be with Swami. With a heart filled with great sadness and anguish, she pictured Swami's feet in her mind while reciting a whole mala (108 prayer beads) of the Sai Gayatri. Never for an instant did her mind waver from total concentration on Swami's feet, while tears rolled down her cheeks and bathed them. Within two days, a telegram arrived from Swami; it read: "Come for the birthday and attend the conference." Of course, my stepfather voiced no objection, and my mother flew to Prasanthi Nilayam on the wings of the Sai Gayatri:

> Om Sri Sathya Sai Devaya Vidmahe
> Parthi Naathaya Dheemahe
> Tanno Sai Prachodayat

****

My mother and I were, for a long period, very absorbed in various mantras which we investigated and explored with enthusiasm. We had especially rewarding and enlightening experiences with the Sun Gayatri, the Mother of mantras. There was a period in Brindavan when Swami avoided the ladies by erecting a curtain between the front and the back rooms. Consequently, we had to sit behind the curtain, completely deprived of seeing Him unless He chose to come in the back. My mother and I were miserable and we decided this was a good opportunity to test a mantra. Since it was before Shivaratri (time dedicated to the worship of Shiva), we chose to repeat, "Om Namah Shivaya."

We picked a spot isolated from the rest of the ladies, and resolved to repeat the Shiva mantra continuously until Swami came to the back and gave us padnamaskar (permission to touch His feet). We were determined not to move from our spot, no matter what.

Soon, a precious little episode occurred. Something moved both of us to open our eyes. We saw a hand open the curtain just a sliver and then two sparkling, mischievous eyes peeked at us. Before we had time to react and stand up, as that is what is done when Swami enters, He poked His head farther through the curtain and looked both ways like a little boy not wanting to be caught playing a prank. He dashed over to us, letting each of us touch His feet, and then quickly disappeared in a flash behind the curtain. Happy and delighted as we were, there was still the realization that even though Swami had given in and responded to our desire, He was yet teaching us in a playful manner that mantras should not be used for personal gratification but for a higher purpose.

****

In April of 1988, my mother received a beautiful demonstration from Swami confirming how He receives and responds to our prayers. For about two years, at the conclusion of the puja (worship) to the lingam (an ellipsoid shaped stone worshipped as the symbol of creation), my mother would pray for the welfare of the world. At the very end of the prayer, she would ask Swami to bless her and her family: Raja, Diana, Robert, Christina and David, in that order.

At darshan in Brindavan, as soon as she arrived, Swami greeted her, then put His hand on her head and said something she did not understand. He repeated the gesture a few times. Each time He would lightly touch her head and say: "I bless...." (The remainder of the long statement was not discernible to Mother.) Since the procedure was most unusual and took quite a bit of time, my mother was perplexed by the length of the blessing, and wondered what the words were that she could not grasp. After some thought, she concluded it was simply a unique greeting.

The next day at darshan, Swami repeated the whole procedure. He put His hand on her head a few times and again said words she could not understand. A very unique blessing indeed! She was certain now that it had great significance, but what?

On the following day, Swami came over to her at darshan and put His hand on her head once again, and it was obvious He intended to repeat the procedure, but there was to be a difference. This time she heard every word. Touching her head with His hand six times, He said: "I bless you, I bless Raja, I bless Diana, I bless Robert, I bless Christina, I bless David."

In that moment she understood Swami was repeating the names in the exact order that she had said them in her daily prayer. He was acknowledging and fulfilling her prayer! A joyous thrill swept over her and a realization of complete happiness came over her face. At that precise moment, a photographer on the men's side felt compelled to take her picture. This picture (page 138) reveals clearly that this is not the face of a 66-year-old woman, but most certainly the face of light and joy: ageless, and beyond time.

****

We learned the importance of Ganesha, the Hindu god with the elephant head, who is the remover of obstacles. Before bhajans, meditation or any other important event, one prays to Ganesha to remove any impediment that might prevent one's accomplishment. Everywhere in India, there are pictures and statues of Ganesha because it is believed that without his blessing there is little chance for success, either in the spiritual or temporal life. We learned that if his trunk goes to his right, it signifies spiritual success; to his left, worldly success. We purchased only right-trunk Ganeshas, and learned the proper mantras and Sanskrit prayers addressed to him. Since Ganesha is the son of Shiva, my mother had for a year added to the Sanskrit verse which she daily repeated, "...and lead me to the feet of your father."

When she arrived in India that year, Swami's new residence in Brindavan had just been completed, and He took her on a tour of His home. At the end of the tour, He brought her to the main room of the house, where she saw an impressive, life-size statue of Lord Ganesha. Together they stood for a long time in front of the statue. Swami then left her alone and went upstairs, not giving her any indication that she was dismissed, which was unusual. Generally, when Swami leaves, everyone else is expected to do likewise. My mother stood for some time, puzzled, and tried to understand the significance of this incident. In the meantime, one of Swami's attendants came and asked her to leave. She explained that as Swami had not given such indication, she felt she should not leave. After the attendant left, she felt a greater urgency to discover the answer, and went into a deeper meditative state.

Suddenly, it all became crystal clear. She had been praying daily to Ganesha, before whom she now stood, to lead her to the feet of his father: to the place where she now found herself. This was Swami's way of showing her that He had received and was answering her prayer. The moment she understood, Swami returned and, with a twinkle of recognition in His eyes, gave her a long interview at His feet.

JEWELS FROM AFAR

You will understand Me only through My
work, that is why sometimes in order to reveal
who I am, I Myself show you My 'visiting
card' something that you call a miracle.

Sathya Sai Baba

One evening in Brindavan, we were all gathered at Swami's feet, listening with rapt attention as He told us a fascinating story of an artisan's love for Lord Krishna. He described a magnificent gold statue that the artisan had made of his beloved Lord. He said the statue had been designed by divine inspiration. Lord Krishna, Himself, had guided every movement of the artist's hand during its creation.

Suddenly, Swami asked us: "Would you like to see it?" "Oh, yes!" we eagerly answered in unison. Swami waved His hand and in it appeared a resplendent gold statue. Many brilliant precious gems adorned Krishna's head and body. The graceful figure sparkled and glowed as though alive. The precious statue was then passed around, and each person was able to hold and admire it. When it returned to Swami, He held it in His hand a moment. Then it disappeared.

Swami then told us a story about a treaty which India had made with another country. He explained that the entire treaty had been carved on a huge emerald that was presently being kept in the same museum as the Krishna statue. "I will get it for you," He said. When he stopped waving His hand, there appeared in His palm a very large emerald. We were all breathless! What an extraordinary, magical evening this was! We passed the emerald among ourselves slowly, not wanting these rare moments to end.

"Pass it quickly," Swami gently prodded us, "I have to return it to the museum before the guard realizes it is gone."

DREAMS OF SWAMI

*No person can dream of Swami unless Swami
Himself desires it so.*

Sathya Sai Baba

When Swami was not well, my mother would
very often have a premonition of the fact in a dream and
later obtain a confirmation. The dream would be unusually
vivid and would always leave her without any doubt as to
its reality. Shortly before Swami's birthday celebration, she
had one such disturbing dream. In the dream sequence, she
saw Swami putting towels to His head. She awoke very
concerned and with the certainty that Swami had trouble
with His head.

At this time, I was sharing a room with her because
Joel had not come to Prasanthi Nilayam. After morning
darshan, I went to town to buy supplies, and in order to
avoid my mother being disturbed by others, I locked her in
the room with a combination lock from the outside. I did
this so it would appear that we were both out.

That morning, Swami called us for an interview; He sent volunteers to the room to summon us. When they reported back that we were not there, Swami insisted they try again, and paced up and down the veranda while waiting. Finally, one volunteer found me as I was returning from town. She was out of breath from all the running back and forth and said to me in an almost angry tone: "Swami's calling you, hurry, hurry! He has been waiting so long. Where is your mother?"

I rushed to unlock my mother from the room and together we hurried to the mandir (temple). Swami was still pacing up and down. Just before we entered the interview room, Swami made the boys on the veranda roar with laughter when he pointed to us saying: "Daughter locks mother in room and goes to the bazaar!"

In the interview room, I told Swami that my mother had dreamt of His putting towels to His head and asked what it meant. He replied that she was correct. He had been putting cold towels to His head because of a high temperature and very high blood pressure. At that moment, my mother, who is always reserved and respectful, forgot herself and from her heart acted like a troubled, concerned mother. She put one hand on Swami's forehead and with the other took His pulse. "Oh, Swami, you do have a high temperature," she lamented sorrowfully. I was greatly moved by the love that broke the barrier of distinction and difference between master and disciple. At that moment Swami became her child.

Swami explained that He had taken on the high blood pressure of a devotee who could not have survived the attack. Swami's blood pressure was so high, that no ordinary human being could sustain such pressure and live. He added that my mother was able to see such things in her dream because she had a pure heart. Purity is a quality of light, and perhaps that is one of the reasons that Swami gave my mother the name "Jyothi" (light) on her very first trip to India. Swami said that the atma (soul) is a small light in our heart. Knowing this fact contributed to my realization that I have been uniquely fortunate. In addition to the ever present light, I have had as my dearest companion and guide the light of my dear "Jyothi."

Swami ended the interview by telling us that after His birthday we would go to Brindavan. He specified the date when we should have our car ready, and again admonished us to tell no one. Watching Swami, the days before and after His birthday, was agonizing for us who were aware of His condition. He continued His usual schedule without letting anyone know of His malady, and we were not free to reveal it. It's understandable why many were confused: Swami distanced Himself from crowds; He never got close enough so they could touch His feet and there were no interviews. It was unpleasant to listen to self-centered speculation, simply in the imagination of many, knowing the suffering that Swami was enduring out of love for His devotees. When He should have been resting, He continued to carry out His superhuman schedule and gave darshan and happiness to His multitude of devotees.

****

Another very extraordinary dream my mother had about Swami, and sadly which came to pass in 1970, occurred the night before leaving for Goa. Swami had invited a small party of three men and three women to travel with

Him to Goa and be His guests in the palace of the Lt. Governor, Nakul Sen and wife, Indu. (This wonderful lady was to play an important role in a great drama which unfolded in the days to come.)

The night before leaving, my mother, who was sleeping in the interview room of Swami's house in Brindavan, awoke in the early-morning hours with a vivid memory of a most startling dream which approximated a vision.

Swami appeared to her as Krishna. On His blue body were clearly visible the marks of the Avatar. (At that time she was not even aware, that according to the scriptures, the Avatar always bears identifiable marks on His body. She later described them to the pundits who verified that the location and shapes of the marks were accurate.) With His index finger, Krishna drew a circle of light around His own body, which by then had expanded and become as huge as the universe and more brilliant than the sun. His finger and the light abruptly stopped at the appendix.

Instead of being elated at the magnificent vision of Lord Krishna, she was deeply troubled. She interpreted the feeling, which accompanied the dream, to mean that a great event would occur but it would involve much pain. Her instinct was to avoid the trip to Goa but she could not.

In the morning, Swami and the small party of guests left by car for Goa. My mother's disturbed and preoccupied feelings persisted, and she shared her dream with June Schuyler (an American lady whom Swami would playfully call, June-July). June, who wanted to drink in every thrilling moment of the great opportunity to be with Swami, would not hear of anything that might ruin the trip. She brushed off my mother's worry saying that the dream, on the contrary, sounded auspicious to her.

At the palace in Goa, after dinner when all were ready to retire, my mother became alarmed as she took padnamaskar. Swami's feet were ice cold. "Swami is not well?" she immediately asked. Softly, and full of love, He said: "Swami is in pain and suffering from the car ride." He replied in such a tone as if to minimize the seriousness of His condition, but somehow did not succeed and she intuitively grew more concerned.

What followed in the next few days was, in Swami's words, "A situation fatal for all mortals." His appendix burst. The incidents of the fifteen days in Goa are recorded in Professor N. Kasturi's book *Sathyam Shivam Sundaram* (Part 3), where he also included excerpts from June's diary. My mother, at that time, refused to write her experience when asked by Kasturi as she felt she could not recount the most painful and agonizing time she had ever spent with Swami. She told me how she and June spent their days crying quietly in Swami's sitting room, with only a curtain dividing them from His bedroom. She heard the hiccup of death and was powerless to help her beloved Swami. Even to this day she finds it difficult to relive that memory.

She felt that Swami had chosen Goa for this incident to occur because Governor and Mrs. Nakul Sen acted as the perfect devotees under all circumstances, and were extremely competent and capable of coping with the myriad problems associated with this critical situation. In spite of the palace having more than 60 servants, she saw the Governor on his knees cleaning Swami's room. Mrs. Nakul Sen acted as a protective mother when doctors wanted to take Swami to the hospital to operate. She stood in front of the door and, with firm conviction, told the doctors they would take her beloved Lord only over her dead body. Not an easy task for her, as twenty-four doctors were consulted in that more than two-week period. When it was mistakenly announced over the radio that Swami had died, telegrams and phone calls poured in from all over India. It became quite a drama, but in spite of the critical circumstances, the devotion, composure and total absorption of Governor and Mrs. Nakul Sen kept everything going quite smoothly. Regardless of what was happening at the palace, the Governor's duties could not be canceled and so garden parties with the Cardinal of Goa, and other official business went on in the usual fashion.

Sometimes, Swami would call Mother, June and Indu to His room and give spiritual discourses of the highest order. He told them how He had to keep His consciousness on a blue light in order to maintain life in His body. He had lost some weight and ate very little. There was an ethereal transparency to His skin and countenance, much different from His usual presence. No other thoughts entered the minds of these three ladies while in His presence, and they were able to keep in tune with Him effortlessly.

Being with Swami in such beautiful surroundings did not feel entirely real at times, but more like an elevated dream-state. Later on, guests were invited for evening bhajans, and even those were quite different due to the palace surroundings; the huge mirrors, golden furniture and rich brocades suggested a fairy tale stage setting.

By the time Swami left Goa, having miraculously recovered from His illness, many "doubting Thomases" became His devotees, including Rakesh, the son of the

Nakul Sens, who soon renounced worldly life to join Swami full time in the ashram.

On December 21, 1970 Swami left Goa by chartered plane. It was my mother's birthday. She felt she had received the most beautiful birthday present of all: that of being seated directly behind Swami on the small, private plane. What a surprise and unexpected present she received upon their arrival in Bombay! Swami invited Mother to be His guest in Dharmakshetra (His residence in Bombay) for a joyous three weeks filled with happy experiences, including the celebration of Christmas and New Year's.

Sai Baba distributing saris in the Poornachandra Auditorium for the 1975 World Conference. The author kneeling, Mother and Christina.

THE BITTER AND THE SWEET

As you remove the husk that covers the rice, so the ignorance that adheres to the mind has to be removed by the frequent application of the abrasive soul inquiry.

Sathya Sai Baba

Great preparations were being made for the 1975 World Conference. Seven gigantic sheds were constructed; hundreds of shelters and tents filled every patch of available space in Prasanthi Nilayam. Five thousand volunteers were on duty day and night, and teams of doctors were stationed in temporary clinics. Kitchens were set up to serve Indian and Western food. Eight thousand delegates from over fifty nations were to attend along with one thousand Bal Vikas children, and hundreds of thousands of visitors were expected.

When one of the large buildings was barely completed (the cement was still wet), we were assigned a room on the ground floor. Swami had told Mother that Raja, my stepfather, would be coming so we had been given two bedrooms. These accommodations were very spacious for only four; some would have to make do with as many as a dozen to a room. We had managed to bring a cot, chair and other items from Bangalore to make the room as comfortable as possible for Raja. We had always treated my elderly Brahmin stepfather with the greatest respect and consideration.

Since my mother had first met Swami, her greatest desire was that my stepfather would also meet Him. Swami encouraged and fanned that desire by saying that one day Raja would come to India. Swami spoke much about him, always extolling his virtues at great length. He had materialized several objects for him, written him personal letters and telegrams, and now at last, Swami said Raja would come to India.

After a few days, when we had settled in the room, Swami came to visit us. He walked through all the rooms and inspected each one, especially admiring the room we had prepared for my stepfather. He materialized vibhuti for all of us and told my mother that Raja would be coming on November 18; one hundred percent certain. We were overjoyed!

On August 29, 1975, the birthday of Lord Krishna that year (also my birthday), Swami inaugurated the opening of the gokulam (dairy). Mother and I attended the official opening but decided to visit again when there were not so many people. We wanted particularly to admire the beautiful Krishna statue and see all the new cows. It was a fifteen-minute walk in the hot sun from the ashram to the dairy. When we arrived, we found there was not another soul around. In spite of the busy preparations for the World Conference, it was unusual that no one would be here.

Suddenly, Swami's car arrived; He was alone except for the driver. It was wonderful! Swami became our guide and took us on a tour of the entire gokulam. He stopped before each cow, and affectionately stroked each one, while explaining where they came from and how many liters of milk each one gave. All the cows came from foreign countries. They did not look at all like the thin Indian cows, but were much larger and heavier. Swami explained that they gave much more milk than the Indian cows, and were expected to supply the ashram, college and schools with an abundance of fresh milk.

We touched His feet in the barn among the cows and the fragrance of hay. We felt transported for a moment, back thousands of years to the time of Krishna's "Gokulam," and standing before us was the charming cowherd boy, Lord Krishna Himself.

Lord Krishna was playing one of His famous lilas when Swami again assured my mother that Raja was coming November 18. Swami added, looking intently at Mother, that it was too hot for her to walk back, so He instructed His driver to take us back to the ashram and return to fetch Him. Mother appeared to be feeling well, but Swami had foreseen that soon she would come down with a serious illness. As He often does before suffering occurs, He softens the blow by pampering and showering extra love on His children.

On November 18, it happened. My mother, broken-hearted because my stepfather did not come, developed double pneumonia. Mother's faith in Swami was unqualified and absolute; but, He had, in her mind, let her down. The grief was too much for her body to bear and it broke down completely. She had a very high temperature, coughed constantly and her lungs filled with water.

Swami sent Doctor Patel to assist Mother. The doctor, seeing the seriousness of her condition, prescribed antibiotics and stated that the water must be removed from the lungs. My mother paid no heed; she threw the pills away and was determined to attend all conferences in the Poornachandra Auditorium.

A miracle happened every time she entered the Poornachandra. She would be feverish, coughing and barely able to walk, but the moment she entered the auditorium all symptoms would completely disappear. While she stayed in the Poornachandra, she felt more alert and better than ever. As soon as she left the hall, the fever, cough and weakness would return and she would collapse. Perhaps a reason she felt so uplifted was that from that time she began hearing the divinely melodious celestial music.

On one of those days in the Poornachandra, she heard over the loudspeaker that Swami had appointed her a Director of the Sathya Sai Baba Council of America: the bitter and the sweet. Swami's relationship with His devotees seems to be much the same as what He predicted would be the course of the Avatar. At first lilas and sweetness. Then, slowly, teachings are introduced and the learning process evolves wherein the concepts taught are assimilated and put into practice. Finally, these are verified and strengthened with tests.

The old-timers told us that no one escapes Swami's tests. They watched many —one by one— either drop away or surmount the tests and become stronger. Of course, we all think that it will never happen to us, or if it does, we feel we could easily overcome any obstacle because our love for Swami is deep and firm.

We often fail to realize that our love, as unshakable as it may seem, is always tainted with ego. Swami's tests very quickly bring our ego to the surface, and upon examination, we will find that our will interferes with divine will.

Our surmounting His tests seems to depend on how serious we are on the spiritual path, how willing we are to be truthful to ourselves, and how quickly we can rid ourselves of self-will and permit God to work His will; which of course, will always advance our spiritual growth. Swami says:

> Give the guru your mind as you would entrust gold to the goldsmith. The guru may need to melt, mold or beat your mind, but do not worry, as He will return to you a precious jewel. Do not say Swami give me peace, but don't give me pain, as Swami may need to inflict pain before the process of purification is completed.

My mother took this lila better than I did. I was angry with Swami for what I felt was unnecessary suffering, much too severe for her already frail body. Whenever I would complain to her about Swami, she would reprimand me and remind me that no one should ever attempt to interpret Swami's actions or words towards another; only the disciple can interpret the master. She would remind me that everything a master does is out of love and purely for the good of His devotee.

She felt a small part of the lesson to be learned by this lila was related to what Swami had told her several times when she worried about my stepfather: "Don't suffer for your husband, suffer for Me." We did learn later that Swami had sent Raja a telegram inviting him to attend the World Conference. Raja had done his best to make arrangements to come, but the plans had fallen through, according to the "Master Plan."

After the World Conference, we returned to Brindavan with Swami. My mother was very weak and still had water in her lungs. She had made plans to return home to Ojai (California) after the conference, and I wanted to accompany her and take Christina with me.

Sai Baba serving food to Mother during a picnic.

WHY FEAR WHEN I AM HERE?

I am always guarding and guiding you, march on; have no fear.

Sathya Sai Baba

Joel was still with Christina and me at Brindavan, but our marital difficulties continued to worsen. Even the pleasure of being with Swami did not ease the pain of being with Joel. Not a day would pass that we did not quarrel and, unfortunately, the heaviest toll fell upon Christina. Her symptoms were quite visible; she was beginning to tear out her hair and was constantly sucking her thumb. I was very concerned but did not understand fully what a negative effect our arguments had on her until I asked Swami about Christina's pulling her hair out. He replied, "You are both fighting."

When I told Joel of my plan to ask Swami's permission to leave with Mother, he suddenly turned the tables on me. Previously, we both had been in full agreement that if Swami gave permission, we would divorce; now, that it came time to act he started to make difficulties. I just could not understand. Then, he told me he wanted to keep Christina. He threatened to call the U.S. Consulate and take any action necessary to prevent my taking her out of the country.

The stress was more than I could bear. One of the major reasons for my leaving him was that I felt he had a damaging and negative effect on Christina. Thus, allowing her to stay with Joel, was out of the question. This conflict and pressure were so unbearable that I entirely forgot to turn to Swami for help and started taking tranquilizers instead. I had never taken this kind of drug before in my life. My mother, alarmed at seeing me in such a condition, decided the situation could not persist and informed Swami how bad things were. Swami stood in front of me and raised His hand in the blessing position, so characteristic of His, and said, "Why fear when I am here?"

The phrase which I had read hundreds of times, suddenly made a tremendous impact; the words went straight to the core of my being. Of course! Why should I be afraid of another person or situation when I am under His care? Let go and let God! I took the "God" tranquilizer and almost immediately calm was restored. Upon regaining my senses, Swami called Mother and me for an interview.

When Swami calls one member of a family for an interview, the others are automatically included. In order to avoid Joel's coming to our interview Swami used some delicate tactics. He arranged to meet us at Mrs. Ratanlal's house so that Joel's feelings would not be hurt if he learned that he was not included.

In the interview, Swami first directed His attention to my mother's health, confirming the diagnosis of double pneumonia and gave advice on improving her health. He then turned to me. He explained how one must try very hard to make a marriage work; divorce is always a last resort. In my case, He said I had tried my best but the marriage was having a very bad effect on Christina, and for her sake it would be better if we divorced. He said I should not be concerned if Joel threatened to take Christina; on the contrary, I should encourage him to take her. If I took that position, Swami assured me, Joel would change his mind. He then gave His blessings and permission for Mother and me to return to the United States.

Everything went smoothly after I took Swami's advice and told Joel he was free to keep Christina. I told him Swami had given me permission to take her back to the States, but I left the choice to him. He immediately changed his mind and suggested I take her. I did not mention divorce but separation, to which he readily agreed, adding that he wanted to stay longer in India.

After three years, I was returning to the West with my daughter, totally dependent upon my mother for food and shelter because Joel had not offered to give me financial assistance and I did not ask. "Why fear when I am here?"

Sai Baba with Christina. To her left, Vidyullatha.

OPENING A CENTER

*Everyone is eager to be happy, everyone thinks
that wanting more and working less to earn
the things wanted, is the quickest way to be
happy. No one tries the other method, wanting less and working more.*

Sathya Sai Baba

When we returned to the States, the first thing I
did was to enroll Christina in school. I selected a Christian
school as I felt a religious background was essential. Swami
had given her a locket with His portrait, but to avoid the
possibility of the other children making fun of her, I foolishly
replaced Swami's locket with a beautiful portrait of the
Virgin Mary. I felt it to be more appropriate for a Christian
school.

On her very first day at school, Christina broke her
wrist on the playground. I got the message and immediately
replaced the Virgin Mary with Swami's protective locket. I
instructed her to take the middle path; not to hide anything
or flaunt anything, but simply answer, if asked, that she was
wearing the portrait of her teacher. I gave the same instruc-

165

tions to my son David, ten years later, when he was in kindergarten. But, being a very bold little fellow, when he was asked whose portrait he was wearing he replied, "Do you know who created you?" "Yes, God did," the teacher replied. "Well, that's who this is." I never needed to protect him from the opinions of anyone.

My mother was still in a very weak condition and the water in her lungs had not been absorbed. She was not able to take a moments rest, as immediately after I enrolled Christina in school, I fell ill. For weeks my temperature was over 104 degrees F. A strange condition developed on my legs; they were raw and bright red and looked as though every blood vessel had broken. I realized Mother was collapsing from exhaustion and I was determined to relieve her as soon as I got well enough.

I needed a part-time job and a place to live, but I could not bring myself to pray for Swami's help. This has been an inner struggle with me from the beginning. Swami says it is our duty to ask God for help, giving the analogy of the mother who gives the child food when he asks for it. On the other hand, He warns, "Be careful what you ask for; you might get it." I have always believed that He knows what I want, but will give me what I need, or is best for me, if I do not ask. Since we are often too ignorant to know either (what we need and what is best for us), I believed it was better to keep quiet and wait.

After being three years in the ashram, I dreaded the idea of working in an office and having to interact with the world again. Just the thought of such an atmosphere was suffocating. I did not feel ready to practice Swami's words to me: "Don't make the distinction, this is worldly, this is spiritual. There is no world, no spirit. All are the same. All is God." He spared me from having to put this teaching into practice before I was ready, and kept me sheltered until I was better prepared.

I answered only one advertisement in an Ojai newspaper (I was now living in Ojai, California) and landed a truly heavenly job. My office was nestled in a grove of walnut trees 12 miles from town. Total silence and a most loving cat were my companions. The owners of the greeting card company I managed were religious people who became interested in Swami, and later even designed and printed greeting cards bearing Swami's quotations.

I found a very small apartment and was able, on my part-time salary, to support myself and Christina. Now with some of the financial and physical requirements provided for, I had a desire to do something for Swami in Ojai where a number of His devotees lived. They would gather at private homes and sing bhajans, but there was no official Sai Center. Swami has never permitted publicity, and even now, many people in the West still have not heard of Him. I wanted to make available Swami's books and teachings to searching souls so they could share in the happiness, peace and fulfillment of the purpose of life that I had found with Swami.

I sent a telegram to Swami requesting His permission to open a Sai Center in Ojai, and upon receiving an affirmative reply, I applied for official accreditation. A devotee offered to finance the rent for space in a beautiful building in Ojai. Three-quarters of the room was converted into a bhajan hall and served for devotional singing, lectures and meditation. We partitioned off the remainder and made it into a fully stocked bookstore, carrying all available books on Sai Baba. The bookstore was open during the daytime, and a lending library was available to anyone not able to purchase books. Those interested could borrow books, read them there or take them home. The bhajan room was available for anyone to use for meditation during the day.

There was much enthusiasm among all devotees at the beginning. Everyone pitched in: some built bookcases or made drapes, while others ordered books and took inventory. With minimum expense, we purchased chairs, rugs, a desk and other office equipment.

We used silk saris, that Swami had given my mother and me, to decorate the altar and Swami's chair. In the meantime Swami sent, through a devotee, His robe for the Ojai Center which was always draped on His chair, and strongly exuded His presence. Mother made a pillow with material from her wedding dress, and lovingly placed it at the foot of Swami's chair. What a wonder and delight we all felt when one evening during bhajans Swami left His footprints clearly indented and visible for all to see on that blessed pillow!

We usually met twice a week and the Center was filled to capacity. The bhajans and the atmosphere were wonderful but, very quickly the work that devotees had so enthusiastically begun, started to deteriorate. We needed volunteers to staff the bookstore during the day. The room and the altar had to be cleaned, books ordered, inventory kept and fresh flowers arranged. Soon, people became unwilling to take responsibilities, and Mother found herself sitting the entire day in the bookstore. When I finished work, I was able to help but circumstances were becoming very difficult for me also. Joel had returned from India and I had started divorce proceedings.

Joel returned in a very bad state; he was very weak from what he said was the aftermath of malaria. The disease had left terrible scars on his body, and his condition was most pitiful. My sorrow for him was great and I could not bring myself to leave him. Being in such poor physical condition, he appeared kinder and more understanding, and because he was also expressing genuine interest in spiritual matters, I thought he might have changed. I was willing to forgive and welcomed every opportunity for this marriage to succeed.

At this time, my mother was planning to leave for India. Conditions worsened when Joel began putting pressure on me for spending so much time at the Center. No one could be found who was willing to work; all just wanted to sing bhajans. Then an event took place which we considered to be a divine sign. A limb from a huge oak tree fell on the roof of the Center during a storm. The Center was flooded and would require total reconstruction, which included a complete roof. We understood that it was time to dissolve the Center. Just to sing bhajans, devotees could meet in private homes involving no expense and much less work. The idea of a bookstore was done for the public, and obviously, this was not the most opportune time to expose Swami and His teachings before we, ourselves, had learned unity, spirit of sacrifice and meaning of service.

Sai Baba with the Jyothi lingam. Story next page.

THE FLOWER AND THE LINGAM

Just as OM is the verbal symbol of God, the lingam is the symbolic form of the Godhead. Lingam symbolizes the goal of life.

Sathya Sai Baba

Mother and I were taking a long walk through the fields one day in Ojai. As usual, our conversation was about Swami. But on that day our reminiscences, instead of making us joyful, brought deep sadness and pangs of separation. We missed Swami terribly and were pining away.

Suddenly, we were both stopped in our tracks by the most lovely, lavender-blue flower that had suddenly fallen at our feet. We gently picked up this most delicate orchid-like flower, and almost immediately its beauty and fragrance brightened our spirits. We rushed home so we could put the flower in water and prolong yet another memory of Swami as long as possible. We decided the best place to put this flower was next to my mother's lingam, which she worshiped daily.

Each day, Mother cut the stem a little shorter, inwardly grieving that the life span of the flower was diminishing. And every morning, for about ten days, I would go and admire the little flower, all the while wondering how it could stay so perfect so long We speculated and fantasized that perhaps, due to our intense desire, it might last forever. Of course we had no idea Swami was listening to our childish talk, but I am sure He heard our shrieks of delight when one morning we discovered the divine flower (at the base of the lingam) had turned to cloth! The story of that lingam is another wonder.

During Shavaratri in 1974, we watched Swami produce a most extraordinary and brilliant lingam: the Jyothi lingam. This lingam changed colors every 10 minutes and radiated a powerful electrical presence as He held it up and walked around the Poornachandra Auditorium for all to see.

In the morning, following the production of the lingam, Swami gave a discourse of historical importance that made a profound impact on all those present. We gasped in unison at Swami's declaration which He made twice, *"You who have experienced the sublimity and splendor of this divine event, have acquired thereby, merit enormous enough to save you from the cycle of birth and death."* None of us could believe our good fortune.

My mother, that day, immediately developed a great fascination and attraction to the lingam. During a private interview soon after, she questioned Swami about the lingam. After His full explanation and elaborate clarification

on the spiritual significance of the lingam, He added enthusiastically that He would give her one. She prepared
herself to receive it by going to the pundit in Prasanthi
Nilayam to learn about the abisheka puja (an elaborate
ceremony, which includes bathing the lingam and is necessary for proper worship).

One day, in Brindavan, while Mother was sitting in
Swami's house and mentally practicing all the steps of the
puja (worship), Swami came over to her and whispered that
she should go on doing "mental puja," as it is far superior
to physical puja. The other ladies looked surprised at
Swami's whispering; they did not understand that He did
that out of regard for my mother, who considers devotional
matters very private and always keeps them sacred and
secret.

She understood from what Swami said that He
would not give her a lingam. Mother said she was somewhat relieved, as having a lingam is a serious responsibility;
one cannot, even for a day, omit doing the puja as the lingam
is a living being, nurtured and kept alive by the worship.

Strangely enough, while going through some boxes
in our house in Brindavan she found a beautiful little lingam
which she liked very much, and she started doing arathi
(waving the flame) to it daily. Nine years later Swami
materialized an exact replica of that lingam for Mother. The
color and markings are identical.

Swami's instruction for puja, which included bathing
the lingam in milk (the milk to be shared with her husband),
was a simplified version of the long, elaborate ritual she had
learned from the pundit. She is now very content with her
lingam and no longer regards it as a responsibility, but

rather a sacred, daily communion that greatly uplifts the spirit. Mother considers the lingam to be her greatest link with Swami.

Sai Baba with Mother in New Delhi.

THE BLESSINGS OF SHIVA

*To communicate one's experience of the God-
head, words are inadequate; in fact, even the
attempt is beyond the fortunate sage.*

Sathya Sai Baba

A miraculous Shivaratri event occurred to Mother
following the production of the lingam; it took place as
Swami walked around the entire Poornachandra sprinkling
everyone with sacred water. She was sitting in the very
front row next to her friend Prithvi, the Maharani of Jindh.
As she looked towards the very back of the auditorium, she
saw that Swami had just finished the sprinkling ceremony.
Feeling very sad and left out, she said to Prithvi, "Look, we
are sitting in the very front and we did not get even one drop
of sacred water!"

As soon as she made that declaration, a huge drop of
water fell on the ring finger of her right hand. Very
surprised, she showed the drop to Prithvi. They both looked
at the ceiling, and then all around them, but saw nothing,
nor did any more drops appear.

The next day, as Swami sat in His chair in the Poor-nachandra during bhajans, my mother was looking at Him, when she saw Swami's face slowly transforming into what she believed to be the great god of Shiva. He was majestic and imposing with an aquiline nose and strange, oblong headgear. Sparkling blue lights were streaming from His eyes and hands. She continued to observe the extraordinary phenomenon with a great sense of reverence, being spiritually uplifted, until the bhajans ended. As soon as the bhajans concluded and Swami went behind the curtain on the stage, Mr. Kutumbarao came searching for Mother and Ambika (the daughter of Mrs. Nakul Sen who had given a magnificent talk in the hall that day).

Swami called the two ladies for an interview behind the stage. During the interview, Swami materialized a diamond ring for Ambika. For my mother, He materialized a large panchaloha (five metals) ring with His and Shiva's images which He slipped on the ring finger of her right hand exactly where the drop of water had fallen!

KEEP GOOD COMPANY

Give up the company of the worldly minded, the association with those infected by asuric (evil) qualities. Keep away from every type of wrong doing. Seek always the company of the wise, the good. Take refuge in Narayana (God); He the Pure One, is the Embodiment of peace, of happiness and knowledge.

Sathya Sai Baba

Over the years, Mother and I have learned that we must choose our friends and acquaintances with great care. We react in different ways: she often picks up the physical ailments of a person (because of her great sympathy), while I develop mental pressures and confusion. We do not take lightly Swami's admonition, "Keep satsang (good company) at the cost of your life."

To illustrate, she and I had been going to lunch once a week for some time to the home of two old friends of the family. Even though we did not consider them to be good company, we just did not have the courage to refuse because they were such nice ladies. Besides, what harm could the visits possibly do us? we conjectured. On this particular day of our luncheon, we drove up to the ladies' estate in my new convertible which I parked in the usual place, in a grove of huge eucalyptus trees.

While eating lunch in the lovely garden covered by an arbor full of fragrant flowers, one friend asked my mother if the pendant she was wearing (in the shape of a fish, inset with rubies, diamonds and pearls) was given to her by Swami. Before Mother could answer, a huge frog jumped down from the arbor and landed squarely on the pendant. In doing so, the frog sprayed the pendant with a sticky, black liquid; and, when Mother looked more closely, she observed two stones had fallen out. Then later upon leaving, I was horrified to see my car entirely covered with black and purple bird droppings, so large, I could only think they must have been made by an entire flock of vultures or other gigantic birds.

These signs were not terribly hard to read and we decided then and there that we would not attend any more lunches. Swami must have been pleased at our resolution, as shortly afterward during meditation, my mother heard Him say clearly, "Monday, the fifth, I will give you something." She thought of many possibilities, but never would have dreamt of what would occur.

On Monday the fifth, she awoke from her afternoon nap with two small rubies in her hand. They were the exact size and cabochon cut of the lost stones in the fish pendant so she was able to repair it. She called immediately to tell me about the miracle and added, "Swami is reminding me of His omnipresence in the minutest detail of our insignificant little lives. How much trouble He takes for our sakes."

Be like the Star which never wavers from the Crescent but is fixed in steady faith.

Sathya Sai Baba

Sai Baba on the stage of the Poornachandra Auditorium with Christina after a school performance.

PRACTICING THE PRESENCE

Be bound to the atma (soul, reality) in you;
take rest and refuge in that, meditate on that,
without interruption. Then, all bonds will
loosen of themselves, for the bond with which
you attach yourself to the Lord or the atma has
the power of unbinding all other bonds.

Sathya Sai Baba

When Mother returned from India, she brought me a message from Swami. The message was to leave Joel. Swami emphasized to her that my marriage was very bad. The day she brought me the message, I received a surge of strength and requested Joel to leave. He gave absolutely no opposition and quietly departed.

The message was clear, but my confusion was great. I had a terrible weakness to overcome: feeling sorry for him. Sympathy always caused confusion and prevented me from doing what was right. The weak mind often deceives us into believing the emotions are correct. Swami confirmed that once when He came to our house in Brindavan, and found me crying and emotionally distraught because of my marriage. "Don't cry," He asked sweetly, with such sympathy and love that I had to stop crying just so He would not appear so worried. "It's only the weak mind," He added. Much effort had to be expended on my part to strengthen this mind. But I was not to accomplish this by forcing it, but rather, by focusing it on God.

Once again I fell prey to sympathy when Joel pleaded to give the marriage another chance, in another state. So, succumbing again to Joel's pleas and promises, we moved to Phoenix, Arizona where he had been offered a job which he quickly lost. We then moved to Idylwild, a magnificent mountain resort in California, where I found a job to supplement the family income.

I found a job working for a cruel man who, I discovered, enjoyed inflicting pain on his patients. The medical field was entirely new to me, yet his expectations and demands could only be performed by a highly trained medical administrator. I found myself bringing home reams of literature which I tried to understand through tears of frustration. Joel's attitude only worsened my anxieties. He had developed a pattern of lying in bed all day with the television blaring. He was unwilling to help with household chores and I felt literally cornered in hell. While in the office, I was constantly insulted and abused; at home, Joel added his share. Where to turn?

Years before, I had heard of the prayer of an ardent devotee of Lord Krishna: "Lord, give me constant pain so that I may never forget thee." This prayer had always before seemed so contrary to reason that it was unacceptable to me. Now, for the first time, I understood its meaning. I had been placed in the most painful of circumstances, with nowhere in the world to turn, so that I would be forced to look inward and place my trust and faith in God.

In this extremity, an interesting phenomenon occurred; the hell I experienced turned out to be a blessing in disguise. It compelled me to turn in the only direction possible, inward, to God, and there I found the peace in the eye of the hurricane. I had to hold on to Him every moment of the day. I would rise before dawn and start to practice the Presence; it was continually reinforced during the day and persisted to my retiring at night. While walking my dog morning and evening in the snow, among the pine trees and in the silent cold of the breathtaking mountains, Diana did not exist. I became part of the universe and was free.

About this time, Joel had a high blood pressure attack and I rushed him to the emergency room of a nearby hospital. He had experienced such an attack before our marriage and I always worried that it might occur again. After he recovered and came home, for the very first time I was able to detach from my concern for him and the condition of his health caused me no further pain. I knew the Divine Presence had penetrated to the root of the problem and removed it. Attachment, fear, pity, all disappeared and were replaced by the strength that comes from right action and impersonal love.

I put Joel completely in Swami's care. I now relegated to Joel the same love that I felt for any of God's children and creatures of this world. The lightness I felt with the lifting of this burden was so exhilarating that I departed happy and smiling. While fervently encouraging Joel with repeated "Jai Sai Ram," I drove away with Christina and the dog and all my belongings packed tightly in my little car.

Sai Baba with Joel and author. To His right are Mother, Mrs. Hislop and Dr. Hislop in Brindavan.

THE EYES OF INFINITY

You are one with the most distant star and the least little blade of grass. You shine as dew on the petal of the rose; you swing from star to star; you are part and parcel of all this manifestation.

Sathya Sai Baba

Once again I returned to my mother's house. She had just returned from India with a letter from Swami to my stepfather. In the letter Swami invited Mother and Raja to attend the 1978 summer course on Indian culture and spirituality to be held in May in Brindavan. I was expecting to take care of the house and dogs while they were in India, when Raja, to our total surprise, announced that Christina and I should go with Mother.

We never argue or forcefully disagree with my step-father, as he commands so much respect due to his great wisdom. This quality automatically brings forth proper behavior from others. We just gently said, "But Swami invited you." In his usual, characteristic way of not letting anyone pry into his thoughts or question his motives, he replied, "It's up to me to interpret Swami's words." I have always suspected that he and Swami have a special code that no one else can decipher, because so far, he has always proven to be right in his very unique interpretations.

Since it was now the end of March, it was necessary to make arrangements hurriedly in order to be in India by April; we hoped to be there well in advance of the summer course preparations. The manner in which Swami greeted us indicated that my stepfather's interpretation had again proven accurate. Swami confirmed that He was expecting Christina and me to accompany my mother instead of Raja.

Shortly after we arrived, Swami came to visit us in our house in Brindavan. He inquired if my divorce was final, which I confirmed. He also wanted to know if Joel was providing support for Christina and me. I had not asked Joel for any kind of support because he implied he had nothing and I believed him. When I answered Swami with "nothing," He exclaimed in a surprised tone, "Nothing! That is not right."

I did not understand until after Joel's death why it was "not right." At the time of the divorce, Joel had no job and no assets. At least, that was what he told me; consequently, it seemed rather futile to pursue the issue of support. Even the divorce I obtained by myself and without a lawyer. With great difficulty I filled out all the necessary papers. Our settlement agreement was simple because there was nothing to divide and we agreed that I have custody of Christina. Why was it not right? I thought. He has nothing and I cannot force him to get a job. What does Swami mean?

Many years later Swami's statement proved, as always, to be correct. After Joel's death, I discovered that he had ample resources to provide support for Christina and me had he been willing.

Swami continued the conversation by expressing concern for Christina, saying she needed a father (she was now seven years old). Then He made a statement that took me by surprise: "Swami will choose your next husband and perform the marriage." I knew He was serious because I experienced, for the first time, an extraordinary state: infinity. I looked in His eyes and they had become as bottomless as a pool of water, as infinite as the space in the sky, so large, that I could dive into them and lose myself to my "true self": eternal love. It was so real that I knew all it took was one leap and I could be THERE.

I was so overcome by this new, intensely real experience, that I did not grasp His words that followed: something about Indian citizenship and Indian husband. By that, I concluded that He would marry me to an Indian citizen. For the next six months, my humorous mother had great fun teasing me. Whenever she would see a very fat, odd or unsightly man, she would nudge me and say, "Maybe that's the one."

I was taking this very seriously because I was determined to train myself to accept in marriage any man that Swami chose. I knew that Swami would give me only what was best for my evolution, and that was all that mattered. Whether I liked him or not was of no importance. I knew all this theoretically, but putting it into practice was not nearly so simple. I was determined to learn to surrender my likes and dislikes and accept cheerfully whomever Swami chose for me. I began immediately by picking the most unappealing, unsightly fellow I could possibly find and then working an attitude-adjustment so, when the time came, I would be able to say sincerely and with all my heart, "Thank you Swami."

I also talked to many Indian women and learned some unpleasant and disquieting information about mothers-in-law. When a woman marries in India, she usually lives with her husband's family, where she comes under the complete domination of the head of the household: his mother. Absolute submission to her will is expected and many of them I heard, were tyrants. Since I started my investigation, I uncovered more and more terrible stories; having to accept the mother-in-law caused more worry than accepting an unappealing husband.

Needless to say, it came as another surprise when, after six months of working on surrendering and finally feeling mentally prepared to accept Swami's choice, Swami told me He would marry me not to an Indian but to a Westerner. This declaration of Swami's made it necessary for me to perform further mental gymnastics in order to readjust. I happily recovered from the mother-in-law trauma and searched for the most unappealing Westerner I could find, thus starting the whole process over again.

CHRISTINA ATTENDS SWAMI'S SCHOOL

Listening makes you learned only. Concentrated meditation on the meaning of the thing heard gives you the fruit of the teaching as intended by the teacher.

Sathya Sai Baba

Preparations were under way for the summer course and Swami asked all the residents in Brindavan to dismiss their servants. It posed great difficulties for us to be without servants and we wondered what to do about Christina's care and meal preparation. Swami graciously solved our problems by inviting Christina to attend the summer course (the only child allowed) and invited us to take our meals in the college dining room.

I enjoyed the May 1978 summer course immensely because every evening Swami gave a discourse on my favorite topic, the *Bhagavata*. For thirty days He spoke of Krishna, Radha, the gopis and many famous figures and saints of the *Bhagavata*.

Each evening the auditorium was filled to capacity for Swami's divine discourse, and to make available one more seat, I had Christina sit on the floor. She would sit next to me on the steps leading down the middle aisle of the auditorium. Without knowing, I had placed her in the most auspicious spot. Often before His discourse, Swami would give darshan while walking about the auditorium. Whenever He went down the middle aisle, He would stop and say a few words to Christina, thus brightening the many hours she sat there.

One afternoon I was feeling very inspired by a talk I had heard previously. Swami walked down the middle aisle and stopped in front of me. Pointing at the stage He said, "Go and talk." I just shook my head, indicating "no" and folded my hands indicating "please," not daring to reply, for fear Swami might insist. I was petrified at the idea of talking before such a large group. Fortunately He did not insist, but walked on after giving me a most mischievous smile. Years later, I vividly remembered His words and they gave me courage when I gave my first public talk about Swami. And I only agreed to give it at that time because I still felt a little guilty for refusing to consent when Swami asked me.

At the conclusion of the summer course, I also watched when a young man ascended the stage and accepted an award from Swami. The award was for attaining the highest score among the Westerners who took the exam at the end of the summer course. So sweetly did Mother Sai hand the award to this devoted young man that I was moved by the love that flowed between them. (At that time, I could never have dreamt this young man was destined to become a great part of my life.) See picture, page 212.

By the end of the summer course, the situation had changed considerably for the ladies allowed in Swami's house. Many more were now residents in Brindavan, and there were many more regulars (ladies who were invited by Swami to come daily). The men were still permitted in the front room, but the women were now shifted to the middle or back room. The back room was very small and dark and usually the residents and old-timers would sit there. Mother, Christina and I, together with other guests would sit in the middle room.

Eventually, the number of women in the middle room grew to such an extent that Swami could no longer walk freely in His house without being surrounded, on all sides, by people constantly pleading for permission to touch His feet, or solve urgent problems. When He gave padnamaskar to the men, the women expected the same; thus, Swami would stand for very long periods while all took their turn.

Just as Swami slowly became less and less accessible to the public, the ladies in Brindavan suffered a similar fate, and little by little, were pushed farther and farther back, finally ending up behind the back room totally out of Swami's view. Swami actually warned us that He would put a curtain in the back room to keep the ladies behind it, and out of view, but no one took Him seriously. The ladies continued going back and forth, accompanied by the loud sound of swishing saris, following Swami's every move. They would rush up asking special permission to touch His feet; they moaned and complained about their problems and begged constantly for help. Sometimes, Swami would imitate their distressed facial expressions and mimic their voices saying: "Swaami, I have soooo maany prooblems."

Their problems never ended, and one day, the curtain went up. That was the beginning of the end, the good days were over. I was fortunate that it did not happen until a few months before I returned to the States in 1979.

****

Soon after the summer course, I had a dream in which Swami told me Christina should go to school in Ooty. Previously, while in Ooty with Swami, He stated that He was planning to purchase the house we were staying in and start a school, but I had heard nothing further until my dream.

I went to Swami's house the following morning wondering if I should ask Him about putting Christina in Ooty —if the school had been started. I arrived very early and encountered an elderly lady whom I had never seen before waiting in the back room. We were the only ones there when Swami came downstairs and walked towards us.

He greeted her very warmly, and as she touched His feet, He looked at me giving an indication that it was all right to speak. "Swami, should I put Christina in your Ooty school?" I asked. "Oh, yes! Do you know who she is?" Swami asked me pointing to the lady. "Mrs. Varma, the principal of the Ooty school. Talk to her and make all the arrangements." I was flabbergasted. How quickly and smoothly things happen around Swami when they are meant to be. But how very slow and difficult things are when one tries to manipulate them or cause them to come to pass. Soon after, I made all the arrangements to enroll Christina in Ooty. When school was due to begin, Swami told Mother and me that He would be going for the school's opening and invited us to come with Him.

A friend of ours, Therese, from Ojai, was in India at the time. My mother wanted her to experience the joy of close contact with Swami so she suggested that we ask Swami's permission to take Therese to Ooty instead of her. We had to be very cautious and use all possible discrimination before asking Swami. How often, in the past, we had tried to help people, only to end up with a very negative experience and instead of being happy they resented our assistance. It is a very odd reaction and a hard lesson to learn, but often we do more harm than good by acting impulsively, or paying no heed to discrimination and foresight.

Sometimes (more so in the ashram where we are all under Swami's direct care), it is presumptuous to think we can help, as if Swami can not do His job but needs our assistance which I often found turns out to be interference. Unless one clearly feels divinely inspired, often the best help one can give is an intense heartfelt prayer.

Repeatedly, Swami has told me, "God is your only friend." Swami's definition of friendship which follows is very hard to meet by human standards:

> *The feeling of friendship must activate every nerve, permeate every blood cell, and purify every emotional wave. It has no place for the slightest trace of egoism. You cannot elevate the companionship which seeks to exploit or fleece for personal benefit, into the noble quality of friendship. Perhaps, the only friend who can pass this rigorous test is God.*

Fortunately, Therese proved to be a true friend; there was no resentment and our friendship remained intact (this was not always true with others). Therese thoroughly enjoyed and sincerely appreciated every moment spent with Swami. We had a wonderful time in Ooty and spent every day sitting quietly in Swami's house where often He took time to talk, joke and make us laugh merrily like those little children enrolled in His school.

Leaving Christina on the last day was very difficult. I had never left her before, nor would I have placed her in boarding school at such a young age had it not been Swami's school. I was very impressed by the discipline, combined with love, that was given to the students. All the staff were devotees and totally dedicated to Swami and His teachings. They did not consider their job as a way to earn a living, but a privilege that allowed them to be of service to God. They taught by their example as well as by word. Ideals were imparted which established a foundation for the morals and principles needed to face unstintingly the challenges and vicissitudes of life.

The students and faculty of Ooty school came to Prasanthi Nilayam for the celebration of Swami's birthday in November. I was waiting to greet the school bus and from a distance recognized Christina. Even from afar, I could see the complete transformation that had come over her face. It was illumined by the most angelic, melting smile; her eyes were full of love. Her behavior and respect towards me was the model of perfection of which every mother dreams. I never could have imagined such a total transformation could take place in such short a time. She would remind us to say prayers before taking food, and then lead us in the "Brahmarpanam" prayer (which is a verse from the *Bhagavad Gita* sung as grace before meals in Swami's schools). She recited lengthy Sanskrit prayers with such an angelic voice full of pure devotion, that I questioned my right to be the mother of such an angel. So great was the change in this little girl.

For Swami's birthday, the Ooty school presented a play in the Poornachandra Auditorium. Christina played the part of a gopi (cowherd girl) and danced gracefully and full of confidence before an audience of thousands. Her acting skills were quite good and in another school production she played the part of Christ so well that Swami commented that she even used the exact gestures of Christ. She was totally Indian by now, and had begun to learn Hindi and absorb local mannerisms and customs. She was especially fond of spicy Indian food, so much so, that after the performance backstage Swami teased her because she was eating too much.

Later, I learned of many instances at school which demonstrated how the tremendous dedication and love of her teachers were responsible for the beautiful change that occurred in her. On one occasion, Christina had a very high temperature. Her teacher, Muni (currently the principal at Swami's primary school in Puttaparthi), administered a huge dose of dedicated love; she stayed up all night holding Christina's hand, while reciting the "Sai Gayatri" nonstop. By morning the temperature had gone.

Another time, Christina fell and knocked out a front tooth. The teacher immediately picked up the tooth from the ground and stuck it back in her bleeding mouth. All the while, holding the tooth in place, she repeated in prayer, "Sai Ram, Sai Ram, Sai Ram." Because of the teacher's quick thinking, love and true concern, Christina's permanent tooth was saved. But of greater importance, her young, pure spirit was molded and preserved so it could blossom into a jewel.

Sai Baba with Christina at His Ooty School.

THE ROSE

Make your life a rose that speaks silently in the language of fragrance.

Sathya Sai Baba

While Christina was away at school, a former problem returned to plague me. Shortly after Christina's birth, I developed a painful recurring condition; my right shoulder would repeatedly go out of place, causing me considerable pain and restriction of movement.

In America, a reputable chiropractor would be able to put it back in place, and within a few days the pain and restriction would cease. Since this happened every few months before Joel and I left the States to live in India, my chiropractor taught Joel how to adjust the shoulder, as we knew chiropractic treatment was not available in India.

Now the shoulder had gone out again and the pain increased with time. It became so severe that I could not even lift my right arm and, out of desperation, I started taking pain killers. So intense was my discomfort that whenever I saw new faces and groups in the ashram I would ask if by chance there was a chiropractor among them; I never found one.

One day, a very charming and energetic young Western lady introduced herself to me. She told me this was her first visit to Swami, and since she heard that I had been there many years she wanted information and advice from me.

I have observed in myself, and in others, that we have a dreadful habit of justifying ourselves. We hear the truth from Swami, but when it comes time to apply it, we make excuses like,"That is not pertinent in this situation. This is an exceptional case." Or even worse and more deceiving, we decide that God is the motivator and since He is willing a situation to exist, it must be all right. We have the conceit to conclude that we have surrendered our egos and have become perfect instruments of His will. It certainly is easier, takes no effort and justifies all our irrational actions.

So it was that I found myself conveniently applying that very justification in this instance, especially when I learned my new acquaintance was a healer. How wonderful, I thought: Swami has sent me such a nice lady to heal my shoulder! And, she did. She would lay hands on my shoulder and I would feel heat and a tingling sensation penetrate the area, and the pain would go. The next day, the pain returned. She would give me another treatment and again the pain left, but never permanently. So, the treatments were becoming a daily ritual.

One day, in a flash, the truth dawned on me. Everything Swami had said and what I had learned while sitting at His feet regarding healers, psychics and people who wanted power, converged in my mind. He said:

Each one's power is within him. By allowing
a weak mind to get control over us, if we begin
running from place to place, when are we
going to get strength of mind? Develop it in
yourself; such spiritual power is in YOU.
God is not external; God is not outside you;
God is inside you.

On another occasion, a woman insisted that she wanted to be a healer and counselor. "Yes, yes," Swami told her. But afterwards He stated privately "If you cannot heal yourself, you cannot heal anyone." People are fascinated with supernatural powers of all kinds, and this suggests that the attribute of self-confidence, that Swami directs us to develop first, is lacking. Also, it shows a lack of faith in Swami who is our very SELF.

When we go to a doctor to help us, we are depending on human power but with healers and psychics, we expect divine power. We want them to be middlemen in our link with God. Swami clearly states that He does not have intermediaries. He does not talk or act through anyone. In going to these people, we hurt ourselves by not allowing God to help us. We hurt ourselves by denying our very foundation and belief that God is within us. By giving our faith to another human being, our faith towards God is weakened. We are admitting that we cannot establish a direct link, and we never will. Since we do not dial God directly, should we expect Him to answer the call?

The moment I reflected and understood these truths, I said good-bye to my healer friend and to all interest or fascination with such phenomena, and started dialing directly. Swami quickly responded and confirmed: "When your faith meets my love, there is a cure."

Back in Brindavan, I was discussing my shoulder with Iris Murphet who is a nurse and has lived in India many years, and she was in a position to give me sound advice. She explained that my only alternative was to see an orthopedic surgeon. The shoulder would be put in a cast on the theory that immobility would give it a chance to heal, or, if that failed, surgery would be considered. Iris added that one of the ladies, whom Swami invited to the house daily, was an orthopedic surgeon. She offered to introduce me to her.

The doctor confirmed everything Iris told me, and I decided to proceed with her method of treatment. I felt some apprehension, as I disagreed with the method and knew all I needed was a proper chiropractic adjustment. I explained to the doctor that I would need Swami's permission before receiving treatment from her. I intended to give Swami a written message the next morning.

The following morning, I stood in the middle room of Swami's house waiting to speak to Him. As I stood, with note in hand, Swami passed by holding a beautiful, pink rose. He looked at me and glanced at the note I was holding. He started walking a few steps towards me before abruptly stopping. With a tender, understanding smile He threw the pink rose to me, then turned and walked away.

All right, I thought, He is not giving permission to go to the doctor. Perhaps I should practice trying to rise above this body consciousness, and not give in to the pain. (Often I have heard Swami give this advice to people in pain.) I was so happy to have the rose; I was thinking of preserving it by pressing it between the pages of a book. It was so beautiful. Pink, the color of love. As I admired its beauty and smelled its delicate, sweet fragrance, faith and love must have met. And in that instant, all the shoulder pain disappeared!

The cure was permanent. To this day, my right shoulder never again became displaced. Simply by throwing me the rose, without laying of hands or anything of the sort, Swami healed me in a most unexpected and uniquely different way.

In recent years I have noticed more and more healers, psychics, and people who claim to communicate with spirits —or even Swami— are coming to the ashram. It is sad to see how they take advantage of the weakness and gullibility of the many ailing, desperate people in order to glorify themselves instead of the Supreme Healer. Swami advises:

> *Any benefit (from a healer) is only a temporary feeling of relief and is not real. If a healing occurs, it is because the person has had a feeling or thought of God. God is within you. From within He heals.*

Swami permits people to discover for themselves. If a person has a strong desire He does not contradict it, as often it has to be worked out. But, in its working out, one may expend great energy and suffer heavy penalties during the learning process.

Sai Baba in His youth.

GIVE UP BAD HABITS

From this moment on give up bad habits, they don't contribute in the least to your good.

Sathya Sai Baba

One morning in Brindavan, we were gathered as usual in the back room, sitting quietly on the floor, waiting for Swami. Verena (a German, single lady) was sitting close to me. When Swami came to give us padnamaskar, He addressed her and said, "Your husband is waiting for you in the bathroom." She was totally bewildered by that statement, and as soon as Swami left she asked Mother and me what could possibly be the meaning of such words. I told her I had no idea, because at the time I could not have told her or anyone that I knew exactly what Swami meant.

When Swami said those words to Verena, simultaneously and telepathically He said to me, "I'm going to marry you to a nonsmoker; you had better stop smoking!" No one knew I was smoking. Even though Brindavan was not at that time an ashram like Prasanthi Nilayam and did not have stringent rules, among devotees smoking was frowned upon. I was trying desperately to stop and had cut back to just a few cigarettes a day but found it impossible to give them up altogether. I was smoking in the bathroom.

Swami, not wanting to embarrass me, delicately spoke to Verena and without even glancing at me, conveyed fully His message, and along with it His grace. I say grace with full conviction, because many times the phrase, "It's Swami's grace" is so superficially used and abused that it seems a way of describing a genie popping out of a bottle to instantly gratify the whims of its master.

In this case, after years of battling with a habit that I disliked but could not give up, just hearing Swami's words was enough for me to give up the habit instantly without even a struggle. My being able to do this is visible and positive proof that it was not through my effort or doing, but undoubtedly through His grace.

As are many smokers, I was basically a workaholic and became very restless after I quit smoking. Fortunately, the desire to work was positive and quickly satisfied. The ten-day Dassara festival was approaching and Mrs. Nakul Sen, the head volunteer in charge of seating women in the Poornachandra Auditorium, asked me to take charge of seating the foreigners in a specially reserved section of the hall.

I had a wonderful time and was busy from early morning to late at night because there were many evening performances. Miraculously, during the entire ten-day period I did not encounter a single problem or anyone's disapproval or complaint. Seating can be a very delicate matter which invariably causes disputes and arguments from dissatisfied ladies.

THE MOTHER ALWAYS GIVES

The Lord is the sun and when His rays fall upon your heart, unimpeded by the clouds of egoism, the lotus bud blooms and the petals unfold. Remember, only the buds that are ready will bloom, the rest will have to wait, patiently.

Sathya Sai Baba

Shortly after Dassara, Mother and I discovered that our available funds had dwindled. We had received a check from my stepfather, but could not cash it in Puttaparthi. Since borrowing money was out of the question, we asked Swami's permission to go to Bangalore but He would not grant it.

Within a few days we noticed a commotion after darshan, and it was clear that Swami was leaving. We lined up along the road used by the car and watched Swami's car pull out of the garage. Everyone was saying that the rumor was that Swami was going to Bangalore. We were happy thinking we could go also, cash our check and not miss Swami's darshans in Prasanthi Nilayam. As Swami's car drove past, He looked at us but with His hand motioned for us to stay. What a disappointment, but we had to obey.

Now, the ashram was quickly deserted because everyone left to follow Swami. We decided to turn our dashed hopes into pleasure. Both of us concentrated our attention wholeheartedly on sadhana (spiritual practice). We had recently purchased rudraksha japamalas (the rudraksha bead is associated with Lord Shiva), and we started repeating continuously, mala after mala of the Shiva Gayatri. We planned to do this until Swami returned.

Om Tat Purushaya Vidmahe
Mahadevaya Dheemahe
Tanno Rudrah Prachodayat

Swami was undoubtedly amused and pleased that we obeyed (or, perhaps our sadhana or poverty moved Him) because as soon as He returned, He gave us an envelope on which was written, "With Blessings and Love." Inside the envelope was two thousand rupees (about $200.00). What a surprise! But we considered the money, because it came from Swami's hand, as precious and did not spend it.

We sentimental ladies went without basic necessities in order not to spend the two thousand rupees, and when Swami went to Bangalore again we were able to cash our check. Immediately after cashing the check, we tried to give the money back to Swami but He would not accept it. He reminded us that in the family, one does not return what is given with love. Instead He said, pointing to His feet, "Take padnamaskar, the Mother is giving."

DOWN PAIN

There is in this world no austerity higher than fortitude, no happiness greater than content- ment, no punya (deed) holier than mercy, no weapon more effective than patience.

Sathya Sai Baba

That month, October 1978, our friends Victoria and Jack Hislop came for their annual visit to Swami. We always looked forward eagerly to their visit because it meant there would be long sessions of questions and answers with Swami. This time, it did not turn out that way. Instead, I had the opportunity of observing and admiring Jack Hislop's phenomenal character and strength of will, so deserving of Swami's comment years earlier to my mother, "Hislop is my best foreign devotee."

In this instance, Doctor Hislop's physical condition was critical and cause for concern. His urethra had closed and he was not passing urine. Consequently, his bladder was swollen and he was in excruciating pain. We were talking to Jack downstairs in Brindavan shortly before he had sent a note to Swami, informing Him the situation was most severe. He explained all of this to us in his usual calm, smiling manner, never once exhibiting the slightest sign of pain.

Swami sent him to the hospital to undergo various and most painful tests. Shortly after, prostate surgery was performed by one of India's most capable surgeons and one whom Swami had recommended. Not once, through the entire ordeal nor after the surgery while Doctor Hislop was recuperating, did he complain or even wince, showing the least sign of pain. We were so impressed by this display of strength and self-control that we asked him how he accomplished it.

He explained to us that Swami had said, only the pleasant should be shown to others. Why make people unhappy or burden them with your pain, suffering and complaints. It was simply a matter of having consideration for others. As for the excruciating pain, he was able, after twenty-one times of repeating "down pain" to restrain it to the point of being bearable.

Little wonder that Swami prolonged Jack Hislop's life (He later confirmed it), making it possible for him to continue serving as a great example and inspiration for his fellow devotees.

GOOD LUCK SARI

*To say that God is the prime cause of every-
thing is true to a certain extent, but you are
not thrust by Him into an iron cage of destiny
from which there is no escape. He has endowed
you with wisdom and detachment along with
a sense of awe and wonder, and you have to
use these for attaining Him.*

Sathya Sai Baba

One morning, Swami came to the back room of His
house in Brindavan where all were gathered and we noticed
immediately that He was in, what we came to call, His
"super-love mood." Swami is always full of love, but occasionally so much pours from Him that it seems to overflow
in torrents, carrying away all of those present in a river of
bliss. It seems He also needs to express His overflowing love
by giving.

That morning, after He gave all the ladies padnamaskar (all the while displaying melting smile and sweet words),
He took several college boys upstairs to His room. He
returned with each boy holding an armful of His robes. He

then distributed to each of the ladies a robe from the stacks. He did not give them out starting from the top of the pile. Instead, He would look at each lady about to receive the next robe, and then He chose from the stack the color she liked best.

He gave me my favorite color, a burgundy-rose robe, a color that He seldom wears. My mother, who likes silk, received the only silk robe in the lot. Years previously when Swami stopped wearing silk robes, my mother was so disappointed that she asked Swami why He started wearing terry cloth instead of silk. He explained to her that silk was too hot and it was not practical to change robes so often.

Swami's overflowing love so affected us that we too were filled to capacity. We watched as He ascended the stairs once again, gracefully lifting His robe to permit freer movement while climbing the steps and, clutching His robe to our hearts, we felt content to end the morning with this charming sight. Then, to our surprise, Swami returned and the boys were carrying armfuls of His sandals to distribute!

At that moment, there was among us an invisible thread of oneness and total unity as we shared together in silence our joy and gratitude. We experienced the unity of one family, with one Father. The feeling of one family did not stop with, or include only, the ladies in Brindavan, but extended to everyone: the total brotherhood of man. Nor was it limited to joy, excluding sorrow.

It is such a wonderful sensation of expansion, not being limited by just one's own personal feelings, but being able to experience those of others. How many more joys one feels, and of course, how many more sorrows. But, the sorrows seem lessened when shared; while, on the other hand, the joys are multiplied.

My mother and I were told by an old-time devotee that when a sari is given with love and prayers to a friend, that sari will bring good luck to the wearer. We had learned by then, that no matter how strange a premise might sound, we should at least examine it before discarding its validity. Thus it was that we tried it. Whenever we gave a sari to a friend, invariably she would be called for an interview on the day she wore it. It was incredible and unexplainable, but nevertheless it was true. In the States we even gave our friend, Mrs. Porter, a silk sari and let her in on our little secret. She later went to India, and soon after we received a cable which read: "Sari worked, got interview."

Perhaps Swami was teaching us that there is no foolproof system, when after about a dozen successes we experienced a failure. This occurred when a friend arrived in the ashram on her first visit to Swami. Of course, my mother and I were most anxious that she would get an interview. We gave her a sari, asked the volunteers to let her sit in the front row on the day she was leaving, and prayed very hard. In this instance Swami did not see her.

Strangely enough we felt more anguish than she. Later, our friend confided that she knew perfectly well why Swami had not seen her; at the time she was suppressing a dark secret that prompted anxiety and guilt. It is interesting that Swami quickly confirmed—when I asked how He picks people for interview—that He chooses the most urgent cases first. If there are people present with feelings of guilt, He will acknowledge them only after they have taken positive steps to correct themselves.

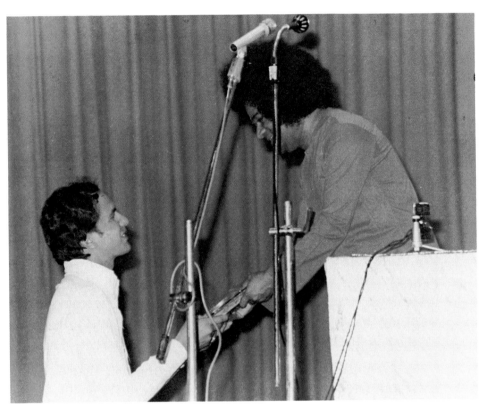

The author's husband, Robert, accepting first prize from Sai Baba at the conclusion of the 1978 summer course. Story page 190.

FIRST INTRODUCTION

*The Lord is all love, so He can be seen only
through love; the moon has to be seen only
through its own light, no other light can il-
lumine the moon.*

Sathya Sai Baba

It was the full moon of Maha Shivaratri (February
1979), a most auspicious day. My mother and I decided to
fast and maintain silence in order to consecrate and reap the
most benefit from the subtle influence of this spiritually
uplifting day. But when Mr. Kutumbarao (retired judge and
ashram administrator) informed us that Swami wanted to
see us, we gladly broke the silence and rushed down to the
interview room.

Doctor Jayalakshmi detected us just moments before
our entering the interview room. She had gathered some
bilva leaves for worship of Lord Shiva (Shivaratri is the time
dedicated to worship of Shiva and the lingam with special
articles such as bilva leaves) and called to us: "What is more
auspicious on this day than placing bilva leaves directly at

the feet of the living Lord Shiva?" Then, she hurriedly placed the leaves in our hands.

In the interview room, we noticed that Swami had called in a small group which included a Western man. After all were seated, Swami called Mother and me to a separate room. We took padnamaskar and I felt a bit awkward placing leaves on His feet. Doctor Jayalakshmi had not time to explain to us exactly what should be done with the leaves. I could not very well leave them there, so hesitantly I removed them, and later returned some to Doctor Jayalakshmi as prasad (blessed, by having touched Swami's feet).

Then Swami, turning to Mother asked, "How did you like that young man?" "What young man?" Mother replied, as she had not noticed the man Swami was referring to. Without further explanation, Swami called the young man into the private interview room with us. "Tell them your name," Swami told him. "Robert," he replied. "What is your profession?" Swami asked him. "Lawyer," Robert answered.

At that moment I recognized Robert as the one who had received the first-prize award from Swami at the summer course a year before. Then, I understood that this was the man Swami had selected to be my husband. I was so grateful that he was not unsightly or unappealing, as was the one I had been mentally prepared for. With a sigh of relief, I mentally thanked Swami and bowed down to touch His feet again.

After a bit of good-humored talk and playfulness (Swami took off Robert's glasses and put them on Himself and played with Robert's ring which Swami had previously materialized), Robert returned to the other room. Swami then turned to my mother and asked, "How do you like him?" "Swami, he looks like a college boy!" she answered. Then, as now, he did in fact look much younger than his age. "No, they are the same age,"(referring to Robert and me) Swami assured her. "This evening, I will send him to your room to talk. You can ask him all the questions about his family and background."

Swami was handling this marriage Indian style by making all the arrangements with my mother, and asking only her approval. He didn't consult me at all, but took, instead, the role of an Indian father which perhaps reflected my desire to be an obedient, Indian daughter. I wanted very much to please Him and had prepared myself to do just that. Adopting this attitude, I also came to a naive, childish conclusion which took me a long time to correct. I concluded at that interview, that if Swami selected Robert for me, Robert must be perfect. I have come to learn that, yes, Robert is perfect for me and my evolution, but not perfect himself. No one is. But I was convinced, at that time, that Robert was perfection personified.

Swami then talked to Robert alone. I did not know then, but Swami was doing His best to convince Robert that marriage was best for him. Although I had seen him only once before when he received an award at the summer course, Robert had been with Swami at the ashram for the past year and a half. During the past year, Swami had been hinting to Robert about marriage and often asked, "Do you want marriage?" To which Robert would reply, "I want to merge."

Robert's professional career as a lawyer was well established in San Francisco, California. Then one day, three years previously, while driving to work, he looked intently at the Golden Gate Bridge shrouded in the still, hazy mist and surrounded by the glistening water. It was strangely different this time; now, a deliberate and introspective musing caused him to see —as well as look at —the extraordinary beauty about him. And while looking across the water, he experienced an expansion of consciousness, a feeling of released freedom which greatly contrasted with his professional and worldly life.

Accompanying all this was an intense yearning to find truth and the purpose of life, and with this yearning, the thought occurred: "What would I do if I had only one year left to live?" His reflections led him to recognize the many things he would not continue to do, and realize acutely the need to pursue a higher purpose in life. He profoundly felt the desire to seek the highest truth. Robert returned to his San Francisco law office and resigned from his job that day.

Soon after, Robert received a book from a friend about Sai Baba and in a short time started, on what was to become, a three-year pilgrimage throughout Southeast Asia. He spent time in Buddhist monasteries in Thailand and Burma and in ashrams in northern India. His final stop, after a year of travel before reaching Sai Baba's ashram, was in Adyar, at the Theosophical Society headquarters. There, he spent one week reading all available books on Shirdi Sai Baba (they had no books about Sathya Sai Baba).

The moment he saw Swami, he knew he had found his long-sought goal, the living teacher who was the embodiment of the highest truth. Now his goal became to devote himself to sadhana (spiritual practice) and realize the self. Robert had left all worldly ties and was free to pursue his goal. The last thing he was expecting from Swami was a suggestion of marriage, which to him could only mean bondage, distractions and a return to everything he had given up.

Swami had seen Robert privately numerous times, and had talked of marriage. But until then, Robert thought and hoped, it was only a symbolical expression. Now, for the first time, he realized it was factual. He feebly protested, asking Swami why marriage was necessary. Swami explained that in this Kali Yuga (age), marriage was the royal road to God. Those from the West have great problems controlling the mind and senses, and even great ones in the East, like Ramakrishna, Aurobindo and Tukaram had wives.

He reminded Robert that He was only suggesting what was best for him out of love, but ultimately Robert was free to decide for himself. Leaving the decision to Robert, Swami added, "If you want marriage, go to their room tonight at six o'clock and talk." Punctually, but with many mental reservations, at six o'clock Robert came to our room. It was a most awkward and unusual meeting for all of us. We had to make the usual polite, small talk expected of strangers meeting for the first time, knowing that soon we could all be family members, but yet, not able to be familiar and comfortable. As I expected, one of the first things Robert wanted was my assurance that I did not smoke which he found absolutely intolerable.

The next morning, Swami called Robert to find out what he thought about me and perhaps to use a bit more persuasion. He knew Robert was confused regarding such an important and permanent commitment. Swami added a little fuel to the fire by telling Robert that I wanted a son, to which Robert lamented, "But Swami, you know I don't want children!" One may well imagine how Robert felt at this time: With great effort, he had sought out and found himself at the feet of his guru, but in addition to the proffered upadesh (teachings), was an unanticipated wife, and perhaps a son.

In the afternoon, Swami asked Mother and me what we thought about Robert. Actually, Swami's concern had more to do with Mother. He did not inquire of me, knowing already that I considered Robert the perfect man come down from heaven. My mother expressed concern about Robert's age, and Swami suggested she talk with him again, but privately. At our first meeting, the conversation centered mostly around Swami, so a second meeting between Mother and Robert would perhaps assist in resolving the uncertainty each felt.

While Mother and Robert had their private talk, I paced nervously up and down the hall outside. When they finished, I had a chance to speak again with Robert, but the time was all too short: I wanted to know so much about him... so many questions to ask. We did manage to have one hour past nine o'clock (the time lights must be turned off), but there was still so much we hadn't said.

In the morning, at darshan, I got a scolding from Swami. It was a sweet scolding, but nevertheless, He reminded me, while shaking His index finger, that I was talking "so late." Then, Swami called Mother alone to talk about Robert, and to tell her that He would be leaving for Brindavan. Shivaratri was approaching and He would talk to us again about the marriage when we were in Brindavan.

I knew I would have no further contact with Robert because we could not speak together in public. Swami had asked all of us to keep this matter private, and though we did, rumors started spreading. Swami told us that people were talking too much, and we understood we had to be extra careful in order not to give further cause.

The fact that Swami rarely speaks of His plans seems to have made people into very keen observers, always extremely alert and observant of His every action. They were able to develop highly sensitive, built-in antennas and often —from bits and pieces of information— were able to expertly and quickly fit the pieces together and, very often, come to amazingly accurate conclusions.

Why so much secrecy? Swami does not always elaborate on the inner, deeper significance of His teachings. He generally does not verbally give esoteric teachings, leaving it to us to investigate and discover the deeper meaning. The length and depth of the inquiry is entirely dependent on our interest and perseverance.

Swami taught us very early that if you want something to succeed, do not talk about it. He, Himself, does not announce His plans until the very last, possible moment. Constantly, He tells us to keep things, including our devotion, sacred and secret. Thought is a power that diminishes when verbalized because of the counter thoughts that immediately arise in the minds of others, causing cross currents, devitalizing and robbing all the strength needed to bring a thought to fruition.

Many times when Swami materializes an object for a person, He will say, "Keep it inside, do not show it." Because the object is full of Swami's magnetism, if others look at it with jealousy, something is inevitably detracted. It now has "the evil eye," as the Indians call it. Since we do not know many of these principles, it's most important that we follow

Swami's words to us implicitly. Later we can make our own investigation.

When Swami told my mother He was going to give her a lingam, she immediately went to a pundit to obtain all the information for its proper worship and maintenance. The pundit confirmed to her, "The Avatar has not come to give instructions on rituals; when He gives a lingam, it's up to the person to find out what to do." In the same way, we have to find out how much we harm ourselves by performing actions which cause people to talk and which can send us enough negative thoughts even to make us ill.

For instance, Robert did not understand why Swami had been ignoring him at darshan in Brindavan for the next several weeks. Only much later, he understood that Swami, out of His protective love, was shielding him from further talk by not drawing people's attention to him. Swami confirmed this to us inside (Brindavan) by telling us He had to wait on the marriage plans until all the talk subsided.

And since I was inside Brindavan and Robert was outside, we had no contact whatsoever, except for Shivaratri night, which was celebrated in the Marriage Hall and insiders as well as outsiders attended. We both stayed awake all night and sang bhajans. He, on the men's side and I, on the women's. Even though we could not talk, we managed to sneak a few subtle, sidelong glances at each other.

My mother and I still had not touched the two thousand rupees that Swami had given. Finally, we felt the marriage would be an important and auspicious enough occasion to warrant spending the money in the cherished, signed envelope, so we bought two beautiful saris in Bangalore before following Swami back to Prasanthi Nilayam.

Robert had left for Sri Lanka in order to renew his visa and returned within a week. The day he returned, Swami called Robert in for another "persuasion" interview. Probably Swami's ignoring and indifference towards him had softened Robert up a bit, because when Swami again asked him if he wanted marriage, Robert answered, "Swami, you are the only One who directs the play. I am content with your recommendation. Perform it whenever you wish."

Swami quickly took him at his word and testing the sincerity of his surrender, answered, "I can call you in tomorrow and do." It seems Robert did not fully mean what he said, or was making the last feeble attempt to be certain, as he replied, "So soon? Swami, I don't feel I know her very well." Then Swami started building me up with praises so dear, that later, when I read the words in Robert's journal, they melted my heart, but obviously not Robert's. Because it would seem that he wanted Swami to do a little more when he said, "Swami, if marriage is best, then you must give me the desire to want marriage with this person."

And so it continued. Again Swami sent Robert to have another talk with me. I did not know Swami had been working so hard at persuading Robert. If I had, I would never have understood why anyone would not immediately want to do what Swami suggested. But then, I had been with Swami for ten years and Robert only two. Even in a lifetime, we can only understand a minute part of this grand, unfathomable Avatar.

Most of us think we are ready to do what Swami tells us, or we think we know what we want. It is such a revelation and indication of growth when Swami puts us to the test, and we can be true to ourselves. Such was the case of a devotee who declared profusely her love and devotion to Swami. When He asked her what she wanted, she replied with great fervor and certainty, "Liberation!" "I will give you liberation now. Are you prepared to give up your life this moment?" Swami asked her. Becoming pale and speechless, the lady lowered her eyes and sat quietly, never to bring up the subject again.

Sai Baba with Robert in Prasanthi Nilayam.

THE MARRIAGE

The secret of liberation lies, not in the mystic formula that is whispered in the ear and rotated on the rosary, it lies in the stepping out into action, the walking forward in practice.

Sathya Sai Baba

The entry in Robert's journal the day after we had our talk, reveals how his breaking the barriers and embracing the first realms of surrender was beginning. He wrote:

"At evening bhajans Swami motioned for me to rise and then told me, settlement on the nineteenth. I asked him what hour, but He said He would tell later.

"It is strange to think that a single event three days hence will irrevocably alter the course of my future life. For years I have been at best ambivalent towards the idea of marriage. Never more than now have I had greater reason to avoid it. For now is a time when I am most intent upon elimination of the control which the web of desires called the MIND exerts over me. Now is hardly the time for me to yield to the natural demands of the mind and senses and enter into

223

a binding liaison with another person. At a time when I yearn most for simplicity, solitude and inner growth I am permitting myself to be catapulted into the complexities of marriage.

"My willingness to engage in such a union might be understandable if it were in the context of a deep overriding love and concern for the other person. But at the moment the relationship is devoid of even a semblance of love or pretence of fondness for one another. As Diana sincerely expressed the situation, but for Swami's interference, she would have no interest in even meeting me, no less getting to know me.

"Yet, both of us are willing to enter into a marriage which neither of us would ever even consider outside this environment. For both of us seek to place total trust and faith in the guidance of Him who we believe is the AVATAR OF THE AGE. In any other environment I would surely have been adjudged incompetent to conduct my affairs.

"At the moment this entire situation has an aura of unreality about it."

Swami did not give us the three-day notice he gave Robert, but called us on the eighteenth to tell us He would perform the marriage on the following day. He asked us whom we wanted to invite, and we gave Him names of some very devoted old-timers whom Swami seldom called for interviews. We felt they were so deserving of Swami's grace (a mistake I have repeatedly made and found so hard to correct. When Swami showers His love on an apparent scoundrel or neglects a seemingly saintly person, I have a tendency to question, instead of being impartial). Swami rejected the names and told us to invite only the Brindavan ladies; there were five of them in residence at that time.

And now our brains became flooded with liquid adrenalin. Having attended many Indian marriages, we knew the countless articles that had to be gathered and meticulously prepared —and there was so little time. Only our best effort is worthy of being offered to our Avatar.

We asked a lady, who was the swiftest and most efficient, to gather the myriad ingredients such as tumeric, kumkum, and rice kernels needed by Swami, who would be acting as pundit by performing the marriage. We were fortunate to find the sweetest volunteer, Saraswati, who kindly offered to string and prepare four fresh garlands.

We were still in need of several baskets of fruit, but after running up and down the small village and visiting all the fruit stalls, for the very first time we found Puttaparthi to be without fruit. Our only alternative was to find a taxi driver who was willing to go to the next larger village, Chikaballapur, and try to locate some. To our great surprise, just as we were making arrangements with the taxi driver, a bullock cart full of grapes pulled up directly in front of us! Immediately we bought several baskets of the fruit and special orange silk cloth to line and cover the baskets so they would be tastefully arranged when presented to Swami.

We weren't finished with this small project yet. In fact it was quite a chore. Now, we took the baskets of grapes back to our room where each bunch had to be carefully washed. In fact, we stayed up much of the night washing and spreading the grapes over towels; every few hours we turned over the fruit until it was perfectly dry.

Swami showed His appreciation for our effort the next day when the baskets were presented to Him. He immediately ordered one basket to be taken upstairs to His dining room. It is true that He teaches us not to work for the reward, or to reap the benefit of our labor, but what joy we experience when the reward is His approval; what greater benefit could one receive?

On March 19, 1979, we (the five Brindavan ladies, my mother and I) gathered together with all our articles, garlands, fruit and trays at afternoon darshan where a huge crowd had assembled. One of the ladies whispered to me, "You know, this could be a big lila!" What a thing to say one hour before the marriage was to take place! She was perfectly right as one can never be certain with Swami. I spent the whole hour contemplating her words, preparing myself for a cancellation and trying to figure out how to "love His uncertainty," as Swami says.

After what felt like hours of pondering and waiting in the extreme heat (March and April are the hottest months of the year), Swami appeared and called us in. The party was joined by two Brindavan men and two friends of Robert. Swami immediately caused all to relax by creating a casual and jovial atmosphere. He said to one lady, "I have a good husband for you, 120 years old!" To another, "I have a husband for you also, 80 years old. Do you want?" Swami then materialized vibhuti which He gave to Robert and me to eat. Then, He gave my mother and me two beautiful silk saris and told us to go in the next room to arrange them. While we were changing, He placed a silk shawl around Robert's shoulders saying it was "an Indian custom."

Though rushed, my mother and I struggled to wrap and pleat our new saris properly. We had to start over several times in order to get the pleats exact, which is quite difficult with new, thick silk. Working swiftly and very much aware that we were keeping Swami waiting added more anxiety to the procedure, as did knowing that Swami expected diligent attention to detail. "Who is the bride?" Swami asked when we came out dressed in the new silk saris. His approval instantly relieved our concern and revitalized us.

Swami next asked Robert and me to sit at the foot of His chair. He then started chanting a beautiful Sanskrit verse in His melodious, divine voice. As we gazed at Him, we felt the atmosphere becoming uplifted, charged with sanctity and love. As He placed His hand tenderly on our heads in blessing, we felt an outpouring of the sweetest love. At the highest point of this divine flow, Swami materialized two gold rings, symbolizing the binding of our union.

He handed one of the rings to me to place on Robert's finger, and the other to Robert to place on mine; of course, they both fit perfectly. Swami then asked for a garland. Instead of thinking why He asked for one and what should be done, I handed it to Him and He garlanded Himself. I felt terrible because of my ignorance and slow thinking; I should have placed the garland upon Him. I was trying too hard to perfect myself, feeling that we have to strive for perfection before we can surrender, as only the flawless is worthy to be offered in surrender to the divine.

"Oh, no!" I exclaimed feeling remorseful that Swami had garlanded Himself. Swami smiled an understanding and forgiving smile, and again waved His hand before a materialization. When He stopped rotating His hand and turned the palm up, He had to join His hands together to hold the ladu (a sweet) He had produced, as the quantity was multiplying so rapidly before us it quickly filled both hands.

After giving us first a piece of the ladu, He offered the rest to my mother to distribute. He then asked, "How is it? Sweet? Life is sweet. Life is love, enjoy it. Life is a game, play it. Life is a song, sing it. Life is a dream, realize it. Life is a challenge, meet it. Life is a chance, avail it."

Addressing me, Swami said, "Next year come with son." He spelled out the letters S-O-N, three times. Addressing both of us, He continued, "Before marriage, he is half body. Before marriage, she is half body. Lady is always left side. Right side is gent's. The gent's body is always the left side of the wife. Now this (pointing to Robert) is half body. This (pointing to me) is half body. Now you have only one body. In Indian philosophy or custom this is called ardhangi. (Ardha means half body.) Wife before marriage is only ardhangi, half body. Now the left side is joined with the right side and you are full body.

"In the future, husband's troubles are wife's troubles and wife's troubles become the husband's. It is like, if one part of the body is paralyzed, the other part of the body feels the paralysis. And so, your wife must feel your pains and you must feel her pains. Both of your pains are removed by Swami. Both of you have Swami. Both husband should help wife and wife should help husband.

"Sometimes, it is natural for you to have anger, ego, temper, tension. You must have adjustment and understanding. First you must understand each other. After that, adjustment will be easy. First understanding. Second adjustment. Ninety percent of people try adjustment first. This is the wrong way around. First understanding.

"The wife must say, 'Oh, my husband is a very good man, very talented man.' The husband must have confidence to say wife has absolutely no doubts.

"Both are Sai devotees. Because both are Sai devotees, you must lead an ideal life. When you go to America, everybody should look at you as an ideal couple and say that you are Sai devotees. Lead an ideal life, happy life, healthy life, long life, peaceful life.

"Your parents, when you go there, must say that you have found a very good wife; a very good daughter-in-law. That is the kind of name Swami wants you to take. This is very important. You must bring good name, good match, good ideals, good judgment.

"Now, she is like a diamond. He is like gold. Without gold, the diamond does not become a jewel. You must have a framework around the diamond, to be able to make it into a jewel. He is like a frame. She is a diamond. If the frame be the ideal family life, the qualities of the diamond will reflect much better. If it is mixed gold, the diamond is not pure. That is why Swami has exchanged rings of pure gold."

Swami then materialized a ring, a wedding band set with twenty-two diamonds, and said, "Complete with diamonds." He handed the ring to Robert for him to place on the ring finger of my right hand, and added, "Always keep it with you. Do not remove it. Sometimes in life, troubles will come. You must develop the power of control. First, the husband must do his duty. First, you must do service with job. Six months in Puttaparthi, six months outside. Independent life. The wife should depend on the husband. This is right. The husband must look after the wife. He is the master. He is like butter. She is like fire. When fire comes close to butter, butter completely melts."

Swami asked Robert, "Now, what do you want? Do you want wife or Swami? Right and left. One side Swami, one side wife. Both are important. Be happy, have a healthy life, peaceful life, long life."

As we touched Swami's feet, He placed His hand over our heads and said, "Good boys." Swami then placed red kumkum powder on my forehead and area where my hair parted. Then, all came forward to touch Swami's feet and the ladies received from Him kumkum on their foreheads.

Swami next drew both of us close and began reciting a Sanskrit prayer. He selected a few words from the prayer for translation. "Putrulu, means have a son," He said. The second phrase, He explained, meant, "Have a long life, happy life, peaceful life. Past is past, forget the past. Be happy. Next year, come with son. I will give Him a name, a good name, a very good name."

Thereafter, Swami materialized rice which He sprinkled over our heads. Robert and I then exchanged garlands. The remaining basket of grapes was offered to Swami. He asked where they came from. When my mother said "Puttaparthi," Swami exclaimed, "Big town!" He plucked a grape from the bunch, feigned placing it in Robert's mouth, but instead popped it in His mouth saying, "Very sweet."

Swami asked me, "Any desires?" I replied, "Devotion." Swami answered, "After son, one hundred percent of your desires will be divine. Before son, part-time devotion.

Unless you have complete one hundred percent faith, you cannot have a son. After son, one hundred percent devotion. Now it's a worldly marriage. Divine son is different. Wisdom is son. Peace is daughter. Love is mother. Truth is father. Devotion is brother. This is spiritual relationship.

"In a worldly relationship, husband is husband, wife is wife, son is son. In a spiritual relationship, wisdom is son, jnana. Peace is daughter, shanti. Love is mother, prema. Truth is father, sathya. Truth and love are divine mother and father."

Addressing Robert, Swami asked, "What is the way to immortality?" Robert replied, "Morality." Swami continued, "Removal of immorality is the only way to immortality. After marriage, worldly life. Enjoy it. After five or six years, then complete devotion. Near and dear. Now we are near. First is near. Near and dear is the negative and positive. She (pointing to me) is negative. He (Robert) is positive."

Swami: What is he doing, your father?
Robert: Business, real estate, selling property.
Swami: What do you want. Do you want practice or business?
Robert: Only to be with you.
Swami: You are a lawyer. LL.B?
Robert: Yes.
Swami: Love of Lord Sai. LL.B, Love of Lord Baba Love is God, live in love. Do you want daughter or son?
Robert: Decide next year Swami.
Swami: It's not right. Decide this year.
Robert: It is your will. You decide.

Swami asked my mother to send a telegram to my stepfather, informing him of the marriage. He instructed Robert and me to go to Ooty and visit Christina after He went to Hyderabad. He said He was planning to go to Hyderabad on tour the twenty-seventh of March. He instructed us to go the next day for a poor feeding, in keeping with the Indian custom of feeding the poor after a marriage ceremony.

Before getting up to grant each person a private interview in the adjoining room, Swami spoke in Hindi to the ladies explaining that throughout the marriage ceremony, Robert had kept his hand on Swami's foot (later Robert placed mine on Swami's other foot). Swami ended the explanation in English saying, "This is real devotion. This is Love."

Swami saw Robert separately for a private interview, then my mother and me alone. At that time, when Robert was not present, Swami told me that after He returned to Brindavan, Robert and I should return to the United States. I knew Robert wanted to stay in India, so I asked Swami if He had told Robert to go back. Swami said He would not tell him, instead He emphatically said twice, "You tell him."

During the entire marriage ceremony, so much love poured from Swami that I felt almost in another dimension. So beautiful and exhilarating was the feeling I experienced, that I must have partially lost my thinking capacity. I failed to take seriously Swami's instructions to tell Robert to return to the States.

When I mentioned to Robert that Swami had told me to tell him that we should leave soon, he believed I had misunderstood. Swami had told him the direct opposite, that he would stay in India. Instead of pursuing the matter, which might have meant being insistent and more assertive, I dropped it and continued playing the role of the submissive, obedient wife I was trying to imitate.

I learned another good lesson. Swami often ridicules the Indians trying to imitate the Western culture by picking up their bad habits. But we never apply it to ourselves and realize that the reverse is also possible; we should not imitate the Indians. No imitation is justified. We have to be ourselves, improve our inner qualities where we are, being who we are.

When Swami told me once that I was one hundred percent Indian, I took it as a compliment, because at that time I was trying so hard to be like one of them. I thought they were far superior to Westerners. Now I realize He was gently mocking me and trying to awaken me to the fact that there is no superior or inferior, and no need to be like anyone else.

5. 4. 88
camp "Porindavan"

Dear Rajagopal! Accept my love and Blessing. How are you? don't worry about your health. GOD is always with you, in you, around you, Be always happy, Bend the body, mend the senses, end the mind This is the process of attaining immortality. where There is faith There is devotion where There is devotion There is purity where There is purity There is GOD where There is GOD There is Bliss.

GOD is with you. You are GOD. why worry? Raja! I am sending prasadam with your wife. She is very worried about your Health she is very good woman!

With Blessings
Baba

THE TEST

Difficulties are created to increase the yearning and to sift the sincere devotee from the rest.

Sathya Sai Baba

Three days after the marriage, at morning bhajans, Swami called Robert forward onto the mandir steps and invited him to touch His feet. Giving him a forlorn look, Swami asked Robert, "Have you forgotten Swami?"

At evening darshan He said to me as He walked by, "Do not forget Swami." I felt a sharp, stabbing inner pain the moment after He spoke those words. I did not have the slightest idea what they meant then, but they turned out to be what I have heard described as the beginning of, "the dark night of the soul."

Swami called my mother separately and told her that there had been too much talk, and He would not be able to see her for a long time. He told her to tell Robert to have a son. Within a few days, Swami returned to Brindavan and we all followed. In the house, Swami continued asking my mother, "Where is your grandson?" But He never spoke to

Robert who was standing outside on the porch with the college students. He ignored and avoided him completely, making it impossible for Robert to obtain clarification about if, and when, we should leave.

We started speculating endlessly about Swami's avoidance, indifference and rejection. What mistakes had we made? Was Swami angry? Should we leave? How can we leave without His permission? Was this one of His famous lilas and tests? The old-timers had warned me that, sooner or later, every sincere devotee had to expect a severe test from Swami. No one is spared. He always tests your weakest points. Many people could not withstand and surmount the testing and ended up at the breaking point, leaving Swami.

I had observed that many of those who fled from Swami had, what I would consider, an unbelievably low threshold for the suffering and tribulation associated with testing. Such was the case of a foreigner who had lived several years in the ashram, and left suddenly in a fitful rage when Swami did not give her a sari while distributing saris to others. Some left and even turned against Swami simply because—after having received attention—they suddenly were ignored. I considered these people childish and lacking commitment. Surely, if this were to happen to me, I could pass with flying colors!

Was this a test? I did not think so at the time, instead I searched for mistakes I might have made. Or, did Swami's behavior towards me have something to do with this stranger to whom He had married me? Had Robert inadvertently made some mistake that caused Swami to ignore us? Such doubts and confusion were not the ideal foundation upon which to start a marriage.

When Swami left for Hyderabad, we went to Ooty to visit Christina. There we found some relief and temporary distraction from the tension, and hoped that when we returned, all would somehow be back to normal. Instead, almost immediately after Swami returned, He unexpectedly departed for Prasanthi Nilayam. Everyone, including Mother, was given permission to follow except Robert and me. Swami told me Prasanthi Nilayam was too hot, and to stay in Brindavan and have a son. As His car drove past me and out the gate, He smiled and held both hands aloft, about a foot apart, indicating a baby.

Since Swami had spoken to me, and by His gesture, had made it clear that we should have a son, I speculated that He wanted us to have this child immediately and then we would find ourselves back in His grace. That was not to be. If anything, our situation worsened. If ignoring can be described as increasing, it increased to the degree that made the next five months seem like five years in solitary confinement —without knowing the reason we were placed there.

We searched all corners and recesses of our minds for reasons and answers, forgetting perhaps that "reason is a bad guide in spiritual matters unless it is rinsed of any tinge of ego," as Swami says. We were willing to do anything in our power (if correction was necessary on our part) to change Swami's behavior towards us. At the same time, we understood that when Swami hurts our feelings, we cannot even have the usual luxury of escape that we have with others: that of feeling sorry for ourselves and considering ourselves as victims. Other people can make mistakes and blame us unjustly, but Swami cannot. We have no choice but to bear the burden, to suffer. And so we suffered. We were in pain as the dark night of the soul descended, and we hoped and waited for the dawn.

I understood intellectually then, to some degree, why Swami sends trials to those who desire to develop spiritually. It's His way of holding up a mirror to us so we can better look at ourselves. None of us really wants to see what's there. We deceive ourselves if we pretend otherwise. How many of us truly want God? Want truth? When we come to Swami searching, eventually He will test the sincerity of our avowed spiritual yearning.

Swami is not at all what most of us wish Him to be. Some may desire only to sit at the feet of a great holy man who radiates love, speaks tender words of solace and consolation, and who gives personal instructions and details about our spiritual practice. Others might look only for one who can boost their egos and, with minimum of effort on their part, perhaps give them a state of everlasting bliss.

Is that what we want from God? It would seem that some do. Listening to complaints of those who flee the ashram upon finding Swami does not conform to their image, we hear: "He did not cure me. He does not give personal instructions. He ignores me. He said He would do such and such, but He did not," and their reasons are endless.

And it is all true. He is not just a holy man who simply radiates love. He is a cosmic Avatar who has come with the full power to take us to our goal, speeding up the process which might take hundreds of lifetimes, by the painful process of burning the only obstacle in the way: our egos. Some of us think we do not have much ego. In those cases, Swami often inflates it to the fullest extent (with flattery and attention), so that when it bursts, one can see how big it really was.

His ways are so subtle and unique, that most of the time, one has the impression He is doing nothing. And then, much later, upon looking back, one marvels at His supreme orchestration of events. Then, you start to see how the most insignificant incident was needed to complete the never-ending enigma of our evolution in His care.

Looking back at those trials, I can now be grateful because they made me take a hard look at myself. How sincere was I? I first came to Swami because I wanted to know the purpose of life. True, but before that, I wanted a solution to my immediate problem. When that was solved, in the back of my mind, I regretted very much not having had an ideal marriage. Swami solved that and found me an ideal husband. I still had a strong desire to have a son. He gave me a son. After he gave me everything He said, "Do not forget Swami," and ignored me.

If Swami had said, "Will you forget Swami?" the burden and decision would have been entirely upon me, and I would have felt completely responsible for failing or passing the test. On the other hand, I could easily cling to the instruction: "Do not forget Swami." For the implication behind these words was full of love and concern and to me they translated into: "Remember, no matter what I do, it is for your good. Do not forget and leave Me."

On the very day I understood the downpour of grace and love that suffering brings, I obtained a confirmation when I read the following:

Question: People have so much suffering, why do
         they have to suffer for so long a time?

Swami: They are being tested, but it should not be called so. It is grace. Those who suffer have my grace. Only through suffering will they be persuaded to turn inward and make the inquiry. And without turning inward and making inquiry they can never escape misery.

Finally, after six grueling months of feeling visibly invisible, Swami gave permission for us to return to the United States. Only fifteen minutes before our departure from Prasanthi Nilayam, did He decide that Mother should return and gave His permission for her to join us. Chaos reigned completely as we rushed about trying to obtain exit visas in the slow-moving bureaucratic Indian government offices, fraught with the usual ubiquitous red tape and long lines.

Even though Swami had been testing us most severely outwardly, His grace was overflowing inwardly. We were aware of His protective hand guiding us every step of the way as events unfolded which could only be described as miraculous.

In Bangalore, we learned that there was a fuel strike. All distribution of aviation fuel had stopped; not one airplane in all of India was able to fly. We learned about the strike from the chief of police while we were in his office trying to obtain an exit visa, which we had not been able to procure in any other office. This added difficulty had come about due to the fact that Mother and I had overstayed our legal time limit in India. We now found ourselves in the office of the highest authority and only he could grant us clearance. When he asked us why we had overstayed, we answered simply, " We stayed to spend time with our guru who now says we should leave."

He must have been a very religious man because he immediately and emphatically said, "If your guru says so, it will be so!" He stamped our paper with his approval and encouraged us, in spite of the fuel strike, to go to the Bangalore airport and try our luck. He intimated that our guru's word would have the power to overcome any obstacle.

We left for the airport with great hope, but were hardly prepared to learn upon arriving that one special plane, reserved exclusively for diplomats and headed for New Delhi, would soon be landing in Bangalore. Robert used all his negotiating skill with the top brass to induce them to let us board the plane. Of course, ultimately, we knew whose persuasive hand and power of word were at work!

Miraculously, later that evening, we left New Delhi aboard the only international flight able to depart from all of India that day.

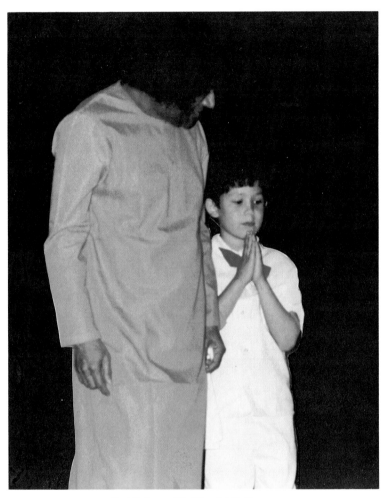

Sai Baba with David Sathya.

DAVID SATHYA IS BORN

*To eliminate the ego, strengthen the belief that
all objects belong to God and you are holding
them on trust. This would prevent pride; it is
also the truth.*

Sathya Sai Baba

We returned sad, dejected and acutely aware of
the separation from our beloved Swami. But life had to go
on and after taking several months to readjust, we settled
in a cozy little house in a secluded area of Los Angeles near
Robert's new office. The manner in which Robert found his
job is interesting; it shows how Swami's guidance and love
are always at work, taking care of the smallest details of our
lives even though we think He might have forgotten us.

Shortly after we were married, I picked up an educational magazine someone had left in the canteen in Prasanthi
Nilayam. I had no interest in the contents but felt compelled
to show it to Robert. In the magazine, Robert read an article
about the newly reorganized Equal Employment Opportunity Commission. In the United States this federal
government agency provides the service of protecting

employees from discrimination by their employers because of such characteristics as race or religious beliefs.

Interestingly enough and long before this, Swami told Robert in one of his very first interviews practically all that would happen in the future —or at least for the next ten years. He said Robert would marry, have a daughter (Christina) and a son. He further added that he would work one year for the government before entering private practice, and he then would do service for Swami. Swami said He would give him all the details of the government work later but, since for months before we left Swami was not speaking to him, in His unique way, the promised details were clearly given to Robert through the article in the magazine.

Reviewing Swami's predictions in his journal, combined with the article in the magazine left in the canteen and his keen interest in civil rights (while a law student), Robert filed an application with the EEOC. In spite of being told there were no positions available, he was called the next day and immediately hired as an Administrative Law Judge.

On April 4, 1980 (Good Friday), my son, David Sathya, was born one minute after the end of Rahukala. But the caesarean section took place right in the middle of Rahukala. I knew that meant difficult times were in store for me. The problems turned out to be much worse than I could have imagined. I experienced excruciating pain and inability to breathe due to dislocated ribs; also I had an almost total loss of hair. There were also great difficulties and pain because of the drying up of the milk supply. Added to this, David had severe colic and cried nonstop day and night for a month, aggravating my already unhealthy nervous state.

We had learned, studied and observed Rahukala in India. In Western countries it is virtually unknown. Rahukala means the inauspicious (or bad) time. The theory is that, during each day, dark spots move in the sun. These spots have a negative effect on our mind and the earth for a minute and a half every day. Since it takes complicated calculations to figure out exactly when that minute and a half occurs, to be safe, an hour and a half each day is regarded as inauspicious.

There is also an auspicious (or good) time, Gulikakala; this period comprises an hour and a half each day which is very favorable. The third, Yamaganda (accident time) for some reason is not observed as much as the other two.

Since Swami Himself observes these times (obviously for our sakes as He is beyond their influences) especially when traveling, scheduling marriages, inaugurations and all other special events, we started to study and observe this theory. A continuous repetition of an incident cannot be labeled as a coincidence. We became convinced of the validity of this theory, after years of checking each time an accident happened, to see if it occurred during Rahukala or Yamaganda.

Some years back, I noticed that President Regan was shot during Yamaganda. Even small things, like falling down or cutting and bruising oneself, will often happen during Rahukala. Devotees are aware that when Swami travels anywhere by car, He will leave before or after, but never during Rahukala.

Once, a new house in Brindavan was inaugurated during Rahukala. Everyone said it was a sure indication that something was bound to go wrong with that house and family. Sure enough, tragedy struck each member of the household, and eventually the house was deserted.

After innumerable proofs throughout twenty years of observation, I am convinced that the theory of the effects on the earth and our minds, due to the spots in the sun, is a fact based on the many great truths revealed by the Indian sages thousands of years ago. Only recently are these theories beginning to be verified and accepted by science in the West.

Rahukala and Gulikakala are given here according to solar time. In those countries that have daylight savings, one hour has to be added.

Rahukala (Inauspicious)			Gulikakala (Auspicious)		
Sunday	4:30	6:00 p.m.	3:00	4:30 p.m.
Monday	7:30	9:00 a.m.	1:30	3:00 p.m.
Tuesday	3:00	4:30 p.m.	12:00	1:30 p.m.
Wednesday	12:00	1:30 p.m.	10:30	12:00 noon
Thursday	1:30	3:00 p.m.	9:00	10:30 a.m.
Friday	10:30	12:00 noon	7:30	9:00 a.m.
Saturday	9:00	10:30 a.m.	6:00	7:30 a.m.

THE TEST CONTINUES

Do not lose faith, seeing some people who have
gone astray, it will be like judging rain water
to be dirty, seeing the stagnant pool. Rain
water is pure, it is the soil that soils it.

Sathya Sai Baba

Our very foundations had been badly shaken by Swami's severe treatment towards us. He meant everything to us, without Him life had little meaning. We lived in constant anticipation of the day we could return to India and reestablish our bond with Him. We waited only until David was old enough to travel before returning to India. When he was only three months old, we felt we should wait no longer. Even though taking David meant enduring greater hardships, reestablishing our relationship with Swami was such a powerful desire that it generated enough force to withstand any adversity.

Due to the colic, David had become allergic to any type of milk other than goat's milk. So, in addition to a suitcase full of diapers and all types of baby paraphernalia,

I added 30 cans of goat's milk to our already overweight luggage.

I remember vividly going to my first darshan in Brindavan, breathless with anticipation and choked with emotion. Upon catching the first glimpse of Swami, I was filled with the hope and trust that my beloved Father would envelope me in His love with a smile of recognition. He walked by...and totally ignored me. As He walked back to His house, I sat numb with David in my arms, holding back the lever that controlled the river of tears that were swelling up so rapidly inside me. This drama continued and Robert and I experienced the same painful repeat performance, day after day, for a lengthy and distressful 30-day period.

There have been innumerable books written about holy men and the lives of saints. One knows, more or less, what to expect from the wise ones and the masters. But, never has there been found a guide or textbook on what to expect from a cosmic Avatar. Some hints are given here and there when we read the life and experiences of the devotees of Swami's previous incarnation as Shirdi Baba, but nothing concrete because the Avatar is as incomprehensible as the universe, and His ways as changing and varied as the clouds in the sky.

Shirdi Baba used to beat people and throw stones and sticks at them. He subjected His close disciples to torturous tests that baffled everyone unless He chose to give explanations, which was not very often. Even when He did, often it only satisfied the intellect temporarily, just enough to silence the questioner.

I have come to the conclusion, that if one is so fortunate as to be with the most exalted teacher one must be prepared to expend the supreme price. This price (killing of the ego) is really not so demanding when one examines the gift (liberation) that He bestows.

As Swami said, the Avatar can be likened to an aircraft which briefly touches down in order to take up passengers from the ground. How to get booking for the limited space? Grace! Consequently, then, believing in Him, loving Him, holding on to Him through any adversity, and keeping Him uppermost in the mind and heart is the effort required in order to tap into His omnipresent grace.

It was an impossible time for me to put any teaching into practice. On our last day at darshan, both Robert and I were seated quite visibly in the front rows which Swami very expertly managed to avoid completely. We felt so broken, beaten and full of pain, that we could not even speak to each other about the ordeal.

Swami had introduced and married us (as far as I know, an unprecedented occurrence for a Westerner) and asked us to have a son. He had bestowed love and attention generously upon us, and now for the second time, He had completely rejected us. You might well imagine the effect which Swami's current behavior was having upon —what we and many others considered —our ideal marriage.

The thread that held us together was our mutual love and devotion towards Swami. How we kept that alive for the next four years, I still do not know. I think the best description of our state was somnambulism. We went through the motions of everyday life automatically and mechanically; our actions and reactions were completely automatic and insensate.

Another devastating blow received during those memorable thirty days was that Christina, after two years in Swami's school in Ooty, would not be allowed to return. The reason given was that the Indian government had just passed a law stating that foreign students could not remain in India if the parents were not residents there. This was a very strange law which I have never heard of since. After much investigation at the time, we concluded it was temporarily written for our benefit by an invisible hand.

Her leaving the school affected Christina deeply, and to this day she does not seem to have fully recovered from those disturbing circumstances. Neither was it much consolation for her to join our despondent family.

THE MOTHER'S EMBRACE

What would you like to be in the hands of the Lord? The flute. Be straight, without crookedness; Be hollow without pride, individuality, will, idea of self; inhale only the breath of God; transmute that breath into melodious music conferring joy of eternity on every fleeting moment.

Sathya Sai Baba

Had Swami not made the next move, we may have lacked the courage to attempt another trip, and we might have remained immobile, lifeless and very unhappy for a much longer time. My mother had made two trips to India during that four-year period and on her last, Swami asked about us and when we were coming. It took us a whole year just to figure out whether that was an invitation, or just a polite question.

Finally, in 1983, we gathered enough courage to make another attempt. This time, we went without David, as I did not want any additional preoccupations. One was all I could handle. Once there, I prepared myself for the worst, and did

251

not go "breathless with expectations" to darshan, but went fully prepared for rejection.

And so it was, that on the second day at darshan, when Swami stood in front of me, motioned for me to go for an interview, and said, "Go," my brain did not register at all, and I immediately turned around to see if I had to move aside to allow someone else to pass but no one moved. Again Swami looked at me, and said, "Go," with more insistence. In disbelief I pointed to myself and asked "Me?" "Yes. Go," He repeated for the third time.

In total shock, and like a character in a slow-motion film, I approached the porch. I did not regain my full senses until inside the interview room when I looked around and recognized all the faces. Swami had called Robert and me in with a group of our long-time friends: the Hislops, the Murphets and the Craxis. At once, I felt joyous as a child among its brothers and sisters, all happily gathered at Mother's feet, waiting anxiously for a wondrous story to be told.

When Swami took us into the adjoining room for a private interview, all the past grieving was forgotten; His love was flowing, elevating and uplifting and it was like old times for me, knowing the link was reestablished. Robert was not so quick to adapt and forget the past suffering. Also, being more cerebral, he needed an explanation from Swami. Swami, with His magnificent sense of humor, turned to me and asked, "Why is he so thin? He is too thin; he does not take proper nourishment (Robert had lost fifteen pounds from sheer grief). He is not happy. Depressed, confused. Why are you confused?"

Robert took this opportunity and replied, "Swami was very severe after the marriage; it caused me much sadness."

Swami replied, "No, Swami was not severe. This was in your mind. Before marriage, Swami saw you, gave advice many times. Gave you many interviews. After marriage, Swami gave freedom and did not interfere, four or five years of freedom. Going, doing your duty for wife and family. YOUR SADNESS AND SUFFERING ARE A SADHANA (spiritual practice). Swami only does what is good for you. Life is a challenge, meet it! You are my instrument. After you do your duty in the world, Swami will take care of you. Swami will give self-realization!"

In the past, Swami had always encouraged me to develop devotion, which I had done by channeling all the love I could gather to Him. Always I had the feeling I did not have enough love, so when He asked me what I wanted, of course I replied "devotion." Swami asked me, "What is devotion?" "Love for God," I replied quickly and sure of my answer.

Swami's words of reply are simple enough when reading them, but to me they made a profound impact because of the expansion of consciousness they stirred. Along with the breaking of personal attachment to Him, devotion evolved into an all inclusive love for humanity.

Swami continued, "But God is everywhere, in everything, in everyone. All your work, the acts that you do, your duty at home towards son and husband, do it with love. See God in everyone. Have your feet in the world, but your mind in the forest." The rest of the interview was filled with personal guidance, family talk and spiritual revelations. We had another interview before we left, in which Swami materialized my favorite "Sai design" medallion for David.

The day we left Prasanthi Nilayam, Swami spoke a few words to Robert in the Poornachandra Auditorium which, within minutes, placed Robert in a state of inexpressible bliss. He became literally incapable of expression and could only smile blissfully as I led him by the hand, like a child, for the next twelve hours, through airports, hotels, customs and all the things he normally handles with great speed and efficiency.

We returned home. By now we had moved from Los Angeles to Ojai, California where Robert had set up private practice (as Swami had predicted), full of enthusiasm and desire to serve Swami to our fullest capacities.

We attended the Ojai Center and when time came for selection of new officers, friends suggested we fill the position and move the Center to our house. We took all this as divine providence, and devoted ourselves eagerly to our new service work. We added a large room to our house to serve as a bhajan and meeting room for Sai activities, and tried many new programs and activities to interest long-time and new devotees who gathered to share Swami's teachings and serve those in need.

Soon after, Robert was given additional responsibilities and appointed as a Director of the Sathya Sai Baba Council of America by Dr. Hislop. Later, in 1988, Swami selected Robert to serve as part of the Executive Committee which administers the American Council.

I could never find the words to express my gratitude to Swami, for having given me such a dear friend and perfect companion to walk with on this path. Robert has truly been my complementary half.

Robert has kept a journal in which he has transcribed, throughout the years, every word that Swami has spoken to us and all of the personal and spiritual teachings that we have received. We have constantly found, referring back to His words, guidance, inspiration and an ever new, enlightening connotation to His words of wisdom.

Cut the "I" feeling clean across and let your ego die on the Cross, to endow on you Eternity.

Sathya Sai Baba

24. 8. 89.
Prasanthi Nilayam

Raja, Accept my love and Blngs.
, I lit the lamp of love. Inside of you
I lit the fire within you. To feed the rage
of lust. of greed, of anger, Bound by strings
of attachment. I whispered to you
The secret of fighting your inner foes
living a life of love, In chanting GOD name
Embedding my picture in your heart
permeating body and Soul with love
The Divine love That you had known not
me filled you with the glory of Thy majesty
Too Taught your breath to hum so (sonum)
That you could see beyond the evil, oh—— love
          with love and Blngs.
Raja, Sai is always with you. in you. around you.
          You are Sai
                              Baba.
Tell my love and Blngs To Mrs. Raja

WHAT ARE YOU?

*This is a human form in which every Divine
entity, every Divine principle, all the names
and forms ascribed by man to God are
manifest. Do not allow doubt to distract you.
If you only install in the altar of your heart
steady faith in my Divinity you can win the
vision of my reality.*

Sathya Sai Baba

Several years ago in the interview room, Swami
asked my son his name. "David Sathya," he replied.
"David is the name of a Jewish king," Swami stated. Looking at me, He then asked: "Are you Jewish?" "No Swami."
"Are you Christian?" Again I answered, "No Swami."
"Then what are you?" Swami asked. I could not answer. I
mentally fumbled through definitions so I could give Him
an answer, but I took so long, He changed the subject.

Why did He ask me that question? I asked myself
later. He knows I am His devotee. I could not have said that
to Him then because I had heard Swami say it is not up to
us to call ourselves devotees, but for Him to say if we meet

the necessary qualifications to be called a devotee. I knew the question had a deeper significance, and for years I would remember His words and attempt to understand His true aim and purpose in asking.

So, much later, while browsing in a bookstore, I was attracted to a book on Tao written by a Taoist master. I purchased it and brought it home. The more I read, the more fascinated I became with the teachings. Within a few days, I became totally immersed and enveloped by the philosophy of Tao. I saw, and was conscious of the "Chi" (energy) everywhere and mentally was parroting all Taoist terminology until I read one of their "guidelines for self-protection," which said: "Do not go to places to which you yourself are not spiritually connected; such visits may cause sickness or death."

This strong statement stirred a response within me and then I remembered and heard Swami's words: " What are you?" His words awakened me and instantly removed the spell of fascination that had very subtly come over me. I realized that one has to remain with one teacher with wholehearted commitment. In fact, Swami once told my husband, Robert, that the greatest failing of His Western devotees was a lack of steady commitment. Dig one deep hole instead of many shallow ones, Swami says. I had forgotten the subtle pitfalls that might lurk when one mixes spiritual energies; this tuning of the mind to another frequency can cause great confusion and come about simply by our reading another type of teaching.

Swami so well describes the relationship between God and His devotee with the analogy that He can be likened to electricity, and we to light bulbs. We all have different voltage and vibrate at various levels. When we are plugged into Swami, He charges us with the proper voltage that our physical frames can handle, and the current flows steadily and smoothly.

Why is it that a person can only survive in "nirvikalpa samadhi" (a very high state of consciousness) for no more than twenty-one days? Because the voltage received in that state is so high, it burns and short-circuits our nervous system. Why is good company so important? Only because positive energy invigorates and restores; while, on the other hand, negative energy penetrates, damages and unbalances our own. What are words? Energy. The stronger the power behind the thought, the more impact the words will have on us. We have often experienced that upon reading only a few of Swami's words they will have the power of stirring our hearts, sharpening the intellect and transforming us.

The most highly evolved beings advise us to be committed to one teacher, not because they consider themselves to be better than others or because they make the distinction of a "superior" or "inferior" teacher, but out of love and protection for the disciple who they know does not have the strength, or the discrimination, "to play" with the very potent, spiritual current.

Then, there are those who dabble or trifle or flit from one teacher to another with no apparent, serious commitment. Those making up this group will invariably say: "All is one," or "Swami is in everyone." The saying "all is one" or advaita (nonduality) is not a concept that can be understood while in a dual state of consciousness, that is, as long as we feel separate from God. We first must become seasoned conduits before we can fully harness and contain "the current." Until then, our fragile systems cannot cope with a plurality of currents.

Often Swami refers to us as "part time" devotees. In worldly situations, a metaphor applies; we cannot expect full benefits if we only work part time. Dear Swami, how patiently He trains us. Year after year, He gently repeats the same things over and over again, just as we do with our children, waiting until the day we mature, wake up and hopefully begin to apply at least a few of His teachings. How subtly He had forewarned me of the things-to-come and how quickly His words —once remembered— had the power to remove the bane of fascination.

Sai Baba signed the front and back of this photo for my stepfather shortly before his dog, Brahma, passed away. Story next page.

BRAHMA

Man has known about everything else, except death. Why should a person die? Of what benefit is it to die? Why does he die? The answer is: in order that he may not die again. He is born, so that he may not get born again.

Sathya Sai Baba

Many years ago my mother had a vivid dream of a beautiful white saluki (an ancient breed of sacred Egyptian dogs worshiped by the Egyptians) standing in the midst of a grassy knoll, bedecked with flowers. When she told me about it, I reminded her that a schoolmate of mine owned the well-known Srinigar Kennels in Beverly Hills, and I could find out if she had a white saluki. When I called, I learned that their two international champions had just had a litter and that these beautiful dogs had recently been in the biblical film, "The Greatest Story Ever Told."

When we saw the puppies, we fell in love with the most beautiful one which was not for sale. My friend must have been moved by our sincere love and affection because she gave him to us with one stipulation. We had to promise to train and show him because he had the potential of becoming a great champion. Also, my friend asked that we name the dog Brahma. According to the pedigree conditions, he had to be named after a Hindu god; his father's name was Rama. My mother was not as enthused as I since the puppy was not white like the one she had seen in the vivid, technicolor dream.

He turned out to be not only perfect physically (I showed him only a few times and obtained his championship), but of extraordinary intelligence and bravery. Brahma had a long life. Actually, his life was extended when Swami advised an operation upon my receiving a telegram in Brindavan from Mother who was in California at the time.

After Brahma died, Mother desired another dog so, as is her practice, she turned over that desire to Swami by asking Him in prayer if she should have another dog. That very night Swami appeared to her in a dream. Out of His body came a graceful, white saluki. Swami played a while with the dog before the saluki disappeared back into His body. He said to my mother, "This is your son."

That morning Robert and I drove to Ojai (we lived in Los Angeles then). During lunch, Mother casually told me the dream, adding that clearly she could have a dog, but she was leaving it up to God to find him. I did not say anything to her then, but as soon as I returned to Los Angeles I busied myself trying to find a white saluki. My schoolmate no longer had any but she gave me numbers to call, and finally I found a lady whose kennel had a full-grown white saluki. She very reluctantly agreed to bring the dog to my house for Mother to see, but she was not eager to sell it.

That night, the lady dreamt that a strange man —with bushy hair— told her to take along another saluki with her. This one, she had no intention of bringing or selling as he was extremely sensitive, and one of which she was most proud. Also, as he was the grandson of the famous champion Brahma (our previous dog), he was most prized.

(My mother had agreed to let Srinigar Kennel mate the former Brahma once a year to international champions flown in from around the world until my stepfather finally stopped that nonsense, calling it undignified.)

When the lady entered our house, she immediately pointed to a large picture of Swami, and asked who He was. With tears in her eyes she told us her dream, adding that this was the first spiritual experience of her life. Then, when Mother and I looked at the two Salukis, she immediately recognized the one in her dream, and I recognized in his eyes the soul of the previous Brahma. We had not one ounce of doubt; it was such a joyous moment to find an old friend. The lady was speechless, and the dog no doubt bewildered, by our expressions of affection and recognition.

This very kind and generous lady actually gave us the dog. She stated she could not take payment for a dog she had not even intended to sell, and one which had brought her such a rare, spiritual experience. We had to call him Brahma because he was our old Brahma. He proved it right from the start by imitating all the things the previous Brahma had done, including refusing to eat unless he was given his food in the same, precise place.

In this incarnation, Brahma became satwic (pure) to the extreme that I would think possible for a dog to attain. Every day, he made the rounds of Swami's pictures in my mother's room, sometimes actually bowing to them or sitting for very long periods just gazing at Swami's face. He loved the fragrance of flowers, and would put his nose delicately into each new rose that bloomed in the garden. Raja, in spite of being a strict Brahmin in many ways, adored him and treated him as a son.

Later, on the auspicious day of the full moon of Shivaratri, I found a wonderful dog which I consider a gift from Swami. She is pure white, both outwardly and inwardly. I named her Shakti (divine energy). Shakti and Brahma were the dearest of friends. They have given my mother and me untold happiness. Every morning, our routine was to walk in the garden of my mother's house with our friends and speak of Swami.

We would watch our friends, totally content and happy in each other's company, never needing to exhibit their joy with noise and commotion as people do. They often taught us to be silent. How many times were the four of us still and quiet, alone and together with nature and God, totally absorbed in the sweetest silence.

My little brother, Brahma, passed away shortly after I wrote his story. Born on the auspicious day of Maha Shivaratri; he lived exactly nine years. He left, as heroically and bravely as he lived, after a painful heart condition which he courageously endured without ever so much as a whimper. The day after he passed away, in sadness and emptiness, an appeal to him poured from my heart:

I loved you
Though we never spoke
How inadequate are words
To express the silent love

That binds two souls
Never was there
A more noble and pure soul
Such as you
Who taught me so much
By your example
You will always be
My inspiration
Can I ever reach
The high ideals
Of Beauty,
Goodness and Truth
Of which you were
A Personification?
My dearest
Through your example
Help me once again
Not to mourn
But to rejoice
Because your death has released
The birth of your immortality
Forever in my heart

Sai Baba with Mother in 1970, Dharmakshetra, Bombay.

MY MOTHER

Mother is Love. Worship the mother as God.

Sathya Sai Baba

My mother is the daughter of a Swiss banker and an Italian aristocrat. She grew up in Berne, the capital of Switzerland.

From early childhood, she had the ability to see the unseen world but could not mention it. The longings for the spirit were not satisfied at home as only conventional religion was mentioned, so the many inner questions slowly became conflicts. Intuitively, she searched for answers in philosophical books and kept her inner balance through the beauty of nature and inspiration of the magnificent Swiss Alps, in whose company alone she spent the happiest times of her childhood.

At the age of eighteen, an early marriage was arranged (as was then the custom in Europe) by her vivacious and restless mother, and she was not too unhappy about it as she sensed a possibility of more freedom, and so it was. Her husband, an Italian industrialist, had a sense of admiration for this young girl, who could finally confide her inner convictions of matters of the spirit that were so refreshingly new. She was certain she had lived many times before because she saw herself in different countries and speaking many strange languages. When she finally found confirmation of the theory of reincarnation, clairvoyance and the law of karma in theosophical books, her real search started with great enthusiasm, and by the age of twenty she started exploring many fields with serious dedication.

After three years of marriage, I was born on a night of extensive bombing in Milan during the second World War. My mother refused to leave the city, which was practically deserted and under artillery fire (most of my relatives were living safely in Switzerland for the duration), because she felt that if her husband was risking his life she would courageously stand by him and risk hers.

During those years, her spirit for justice and service surfaced in full force, and she became involved with the war to her maximum capacity. She found people that were starving and risked her life taking them food. My uncle had an ulcer and she managed to take contraband milk to him (often through machine gun fire) by lying flat in a small rowboat. She hid several Jews in her home at great risk; she could have gone to a concentration camp if they were discovered. For other Jews fleeing certain death, she helped to obtain underground passage out of Italy.

She described to me how war can bring out the best in people because everyone lives each moment as though it were the last. There is no time for petty quarrels. A great spirit of unity develops among people thrown together in underground shelters, waiting and listening to the bombing above. There was a sense of gratitude for life; positive, constructive feelings and heightened awareness emanate from people who put every possible moment to its best use. Spirituality is practiced and lived as in no other time. From this aspect of the war, her adventurous spirit learned much.

When the war ended, there was a period of worldliness and since my father was very wealthy, her worldly desires were quickly satisfied to the extreme. There are those who would say Mother had it all: from a yacht on the Riviera to a luxury penthouse. There were cooks, maids and liveried chauffeurs to drive the luxury cars. A Swiss nurse attended me. French couturiers provided the furs, and the finest shops the jewelry. She very shortly became sated and realized the shallowness and emptiness of her lifestyle.

A tremendous desire for renunciation overtook Mother. She wanted to give everything away, and with only the clothes on her back live the life of a sanyasi (monk) wandering on pilgrimages in search of truth. Her love towards me and a sense of duty created conflicts which my understanding father helped to resolve. For him, too, the worldly life did not mean much and he was intrigued at the idea of exploring new possibilities, but he was not ready to do this entirely without means as he did not feel her pressing urge for total renunciation.

Nevertheless, he took a minimum amount and gave his shares of the family's large chemical factory to his brothers, and in 1949, after my mother gave away all her possessions and distributed much wealth among the poor, we set sail for Chile in South America. Mother took only a minimum of luggage and a few of her favorite books of inspiration: Tagore, Inayatkhan and the *Bhagavad Gita*.

We toured all of Chile by jeep and my parents decided to settle near the banks of a beautiful lake in Villarica. They purchased 50 acres of land and built a charming log house overlooking two snow-capped volcanoes. A foreman's house was built as my father, having also a doctorate in chemistry, intended to grow herbs and extract oils for pharmaceutical use.

Father could not escape for long his destiny to return to business, and soon met an Italian industrialist who presented him with the tempting offer of partnership in a large chemical factory in Sao Paulo, Brazil. And mother, who wanted a life of poverty and renunciation, soon found herself thrown back into the life of luxury, servants and all the paraphernalia she wanted to renounce.

At about that time, she met a most fascinating yogi disguised as a simple caretaker at the Cancer Research Center in Sao Paulo. She immediately noticed his unique penetrating eyes, and the aura of peace that surrounded him; they became acquainted. He told her that his master, with whom he was in telepathic communication, was in the Himalayas and had trained him to acquire every imaginable yogic power, including healing. That is all she needed to hear; Mother immediately brought him all sorts of sick people whom he miraculously cured.

He told her she could develop all the same powers, and gave her exercises to practice which could open these potential centers within her. When she consulted her heart, she realized she could not take him as her teacher as she was not seeking power. In spite of her certainty of his genuineness, that was not the path she chose to follow.

Since my education was always uppermost in her mind and being dissatisfied with the schools in Brazil, Mother decided to bring me to Krishnamurti's school in Ojai, California. She had heard of Krishnamurti's school years previously in Holland, and wanted to enroll me there. For her, a spiritual education was absolutely essential for a child. She had become very interested in Krishnamurti's teachings while in Milan, and had even gone to London to hear his talks. In London, she spoke with Krishnamurti and, for the first time, met his companion and her future husband, Rajagopal. She felt very spiritually uplifted when she looked into Raja's eyes and she never forgot him.

When we arrived in Los Angeles, we stayed at the Biltmore Hotel where Paramahansa Yogananda was giving a lecture. My mother did not know one word of English but had read *Autobiography of a Yogi* in Italian, and felt a link with Sri Yukteshwar (Yogananda's master). She also became interested in the idea of living among a colony of people dedicated to the spiritual life, such as the one Yogananda had established at the Self-Realization Fellowship in Los Angeles, California.

In Ojai, she discovered that I was too young (I was eight years of age at the time) for Krishnamurti's school, and after being recommended to another excellent boarding school in Ojai, I was enrolled there. Mother returned to Sao Paulo, but it saddened her to leave Ojai which captured her spirit immediately. She loved the beautiful Ojai Valley and felt she belonged there.

After sometime of the worldly life she so much wanted to forego, she concluded that the compromise was not working; she was not one bit closer to her goal. She prevailed upon Father to leave South America and the chemical factory, and explore the colony of spiritually minded people at the Self-Realization Fellowship.

They left Brazil and went straight to the headquarters of the S.R.F., not knowing that one had to be a member for years before being allowed to live there. A meeting was arranged for them with Sister Dayamata (who later became the president) and she immediately accepted them as residents. In spiritual matters, my mother has always been quite fortunate in having doors opened for her.

Brother Kriyananda was assigned as their spiritual instructor. (Twenty-one years later, in 1973, she was to meet him again when Brother Kriyananda visited India and sought Sai Baba's guidance and was blessed with an interview.) In the S.R.F. community, my father lived with the brothers and my mother with the sisters. Later, Sister Dayamata again made an exception and allowed me (the only child at the headquarters) to join my mother. Thus it was, at nine years of age, that my first spiritual instructions began. I remember so well trying hard to meditate in the chapel for hours at a time. Instead, I usually fell asleep and blocked the door with my body so everyone had to step over me to exit. Of course I was embarrassed due to my inability to remain awake. The pattern of my daily routine was to join the sisters in the recharging exercises on the patio and prayers in the chapel in the evening. In spite of what I may have considered my spiritual frailties, I enjoyed community life and company of the sisters exceedingly. Their charity and kindness towards me taught many valuable lessons.

Likewise, Father seemed happy and content with our new life. Although Mother had not yet found the spiritual embodiment she perceived to be her bent, our satisfaction and the charity of the good brothers and sisters eased her questionable situation for the present.

She had, very early on, realized that her spiritual progress on this path had reached a stalemate. She attributed this to her soft and sheltered lifestyle, surrounded by luxuries which served only as escape from the realities and vicissitudes of the world. In her mind, she equated hardships and adversity as essential components necessary for growth. She finally expressed her feelings to Sister Dayamata, and with deep gratitude for all the kindness received, we left the S.R.F. to settle in the little village of her dreams, Ojai, California.

Of course Father was with us, but after some time in Ojai, a longing for his country and its customs, and way of living became stronger. He finally realized he would never be able to adjust to the life situation now perceived as quite tenable by Mother. Being a very wise and just man, he believed that both should have the freedom to pursue their different lifestyles unencumbered. Thus it was, with love and friendship intact, my mother and father parted. He returned to Milan where he resumed his life as an industrialist.

I chose to stay with my mother. Together we led a happy and simple life in Ojai for many years. Later I attended Krishnamurti's school for two years, and because of my interest in languages, I studied French and German in Lausanne, Switzerland and attended Cambridge in Milan, Italy. Rajagopal became our dearest friend; in him my mother found spiritual affinity and I, after they were married, a spiritual father whose influence has gently guided me throughout the years.

Mother helped Raja in his editing and publishing of Krishnamurti's books. While helping there, she discovered books about Ramana Maharshi (an Indian saint) which impressed her deeply. At about that time, she developed very serious health problems and was taken in critical condition to the hospital where she was told the prognosis was very bad and an operation was necessary.

Swami, in recent years, confirmed that He entered Mother's life at this point, though she did not have the slightest knowledge about Him at that time. She prayed earnestly with all her heart to Ramana Maharshi, and he appeared to her in a vision when she was fully awake. His face was bathed in a warm, wondrous light; he smiled and touched her on the forehead. She instantly experienced a powerful, spiritual awakening and along with it, a complete physical renewal.

Shortly after, in 1964, she received the first journal of the Ramana Maharshi ashram, in which she read an article about Sai Baba of Shirdi by Arthur Osborne. The simplicity and beauty of the "old man" and his teachings touched her heart, and she prayed to Shirdi Baba to help her find her guru —someone living—as all the ones she loved such as Ramana Maharshi and Ramakrishna were no longer in the body.

She persevered and continued in her prayers for three years, until one day, a friend told her that Sathya Sai Baba was a reincarnation of Shirdi Baba and gave her a cassette tape of Sai Baba singing bhajans. When that same friend invited my mother to join a group going to India to see Sai Baba, my mother had no difficulty obtaining permission from my stepfather to go. Raja had already sensed a unique greatness from the voice on the cassette tape.

The moment my mother saw Sai Baba, she knew her long search had come to an end. She saw and experienced Sai Baba as the divine manifestation of purity, love, perfection and divinity. Her goal from then on became one of surrender, and she placed herself completely in His hands. As the Krishna Avatar promised in the *Bhagavad Gita* to those who surrender, "I shall bear the burden of your welfare here and hereafter," Sai Baba, the present Avatar, has continued to keep that promise towards His devotees.

He has played the role of divine physician and healer towards her on numerous occasions by performing miraculous healings. Once, He materialized sixty pearl-colored pills to be taken for a serious stomach ailment. Another time, thirty coral tablets of unusual shape cured a condition which included a very high temperature. On another occasion, He materialized a solid stick of vibhuti, four inches long and five inches in diameter which had special curative and healing properties; it was also an effective safeguard against all sorts of animal, insect or snake bites.

Also materialized for her were two containers (one brass, one silver) of vibhuti with Swami's initials engraved on the cover. One container was always refilling itself and gave a never-ending supply of vibhuti. Sometimes, He cured Mother in person, as in one case when she arrived in India with the Hislop family. In that instance, He dispelled instantly a serious case of stomach ulcers merely by rubbing her hand.

Other times He gave instructions and cures through dreams. He showed her a sort of T'ai Chi exercise to practice, which within a week relieved completely a painful, long-standing condition in her elbows. He made a chiropractic adjustment to her head while she was asleep. Something had gone out of place and could not be adjusted by any chiropractor because of its location. When Mother awoke, she remembered Swami's adjustment and was grateful to be relieved of all pressure in her head.

Swami invited Mother on many tours with Him throughout India (some lasting as long as six weeks) during which they visited numerous states by car, plane and chartered plane. She was always invited to stay with Him as His guest at the various homes in which He resided. Swami has gently guided her every step of the way on the spiritual path. This has not been a path of roses and glamour, as for the serious aspirant, much work on oneself has to be done which demands maximum endurance, unlimited patience and complete objectivity.

Swami has held a mirror up to Mother so she could see every possible crevice of her character in order to determine where work needed to be done. He was able to do this because she asked and wanted to learn the truth. "Three-fourths inquiry and one-fourth devotion," Swami advised her. Inquiry has opened new horizons, and devotion has opened her heart to such an extent that, within it, there is room for anyone and everyone.

The paths of light-bearers are lonely and silent. In solitude and without exhibition, they give of themselves and shed light on many. Mother has been a brilliant light in my life: a guide and illuminator of the path.

Her countless, extraordinary experiences in the long years of close contact with Swami have given her invaluable insight, so extensive that it would take another book to recount. Perhaps this will be a future project, as I feel much benefit to many would result in sharing the experiences of my dear, "Jyothi."

Remember the Wheel of Cause and Consequence, of Deed and Destiny and the Wheel of Dharma that rights them all.

Sathya Sai Baba

My father, Rajagopal in his youth.

MY FATHER

Father is truth. Worship the father as God.

Sathya Sai Baba

In this chapter I refer to Raja as my father. Although not biologically so, Swami has always called him my father as, in matters of the soul, he has always been a spiritual father for me. My father, Desikacharya Rajagopalacharya, was one of the two Indian boys who Bishop Leadbeater prophesied, "will play an unusual role on the world's stage." The other boy was Jiddu Krishnamurti.

In December 1913, Bishop Leadbeater presided and lectured at the Kerala Theosophical Conference at Calicut, India. The evening before the conference, he was told by his master that he would find one of the master's people. Being extensively and scientifically trained by the Theosophical masters in the proper use of clairvoyance, as soon as he arrived at the conference, he scanned through the members present looking for someone with an unusual aura. Even though he did not find anyone that day, he never doubted his master's words.

The next day he saw a young boy with a magnificent aura and instantly recognized him (Raja). He learned that the boy's father had intended to be present the first day, but at a junction station his cook missed the train. As an Ayyangar Brahmin, he could not accept food from any other Brahmin except an Ayyangar; consequently, he had to travel always with his cook. Owing to this accident, his arrival at the conference was delayed by one day. From then on Raja, together with Krishna (J. Krishnamurti), was under the spiritual care and training of Dr. Annie Besant and Bishop Leadbeater.

Even though they both had the same teachers, they did not meet until many years later in London, where Raja was attending Cambridge (he graduated with honors in law) and Krishna was being carefully groomed to be the much prophesied "World Teacher" if found to be worthy.

They became very good friends in spite of Krishna's initial fear that Raja might be a possible rival for the position of World Teacher. This fear may have been heightened due to Leadbeater's having declared that Raja had been St. Bernard of Clairvaux in his past life, and was destined to become a Buddha in his future life.

Krishnamurti's brother, Nitya, who never enjoyed a robust physical state, developed a critical lung condition and though the serious situation was halted temporarily, he eventually succumbed to the disease. This sad event appears to have initiated an extremely significant effect on all facets of Krishnamurti's life. Until then, he had been in contact with the masters and eagerly shared with many their words of wisdom to him while he was in a sleeping state.

The masters had assured him that Nitya would not die. He believed them with all his heart.

Just as Swami often does, the masters had broken his spirit as well as his heart. He considered the toll they had elicited from him to be so severe that he soon denied them, the Theosophical Society, Bishop Leadbeater and the woman he used to call, "Amma" (Mother), Dr. Annie Besant. It was also rumored that since he previously had been a vehicle through whom the masters spoke —once the forces of good were removed— he was left open to other forces.

Dr. Besant never denied him however and, out of her continued motherly love and deep concern for his future, she asked Raja to promise her that he would always help Krishna, and stay by his side. She felt with deep conviction that without Raja, Krishna could not make it, as he was easily influenced, sensitive and needed Raja's strength and protection.

Indeed, even before Nitya died, Krishna had asked Raja to help him carry on the work as he was the first to recognize what outstanding organizational capacities Raja had. At that time, putting his personal life aside, Raja committed himself totally and selflessly to what was to be for the next 50 years, his "dharma" (duty). He organized "Krishnamurti Writings," with offices all over the world, which published and translated Krishnamurti's talks and teachings into many languages. He organized all of Krishnamurti's talks and established schools in America, India and Europe. So great were his capacities, that Rabindranath Tagore (the well-known Indian poet) sent Raja letters of praise and encouragement for having established three schools by the time he was sixteen years of age. C. Jinarajadasa, former President of the Theosophical

Society said, "Raja had only to propound his scheme and offers of help came. I have always admired and envied this gift of his."

Raja was adamant about not collecting money from people anytime, and most particularly at Krishnamurti's talks. Matters of the spirit could not be bought and sold like merchandise. Only unsolicited donations given with the right attitude and pure motives were ever accepted. One could rarely find a person with such high standards of integrity, both behind the scenes and in full view of the public.

A falling-out ultimately occurred between Raja and Krishna. For very personal reasons, known only by a handful of people, Raja's dearest friend Krishna brought three lawsuits against Raja over the course of fifteen years. All were settled out of court for lack of evidence. In the first lawsuit, Raja did not want even to defend himself against the many false accusations.

Having completely given up any desire for personal, worldly gain such as career and family, and out of high ideals of dedication to truth, he had given himself wholeheartedly and selflessly to spreading the teachings of Krishnamurti; naturally, Raja's heart was broken by this betrayal. Finally, Mother suggested he cable Swami for advice on what action to take. Immediately Swami cabled the following written message: " FIGHT FOR TRUTH TO THE END. DO NOT WORRY. I AM ON YOUR SIDE. BE COURAGEOUS. TRUTH IS GOD. LIVE IN TRUTH."

Raja held fast to the saying: "One with God is a majority," and he had Swami's total support. He took Swami's advice and defended himself by painstakingly gathering evidence, some of which dated back forty years. Raja was still not willing to reveal the true circumstances out of love and protection for Krishna.

Swami materialized a beautiful silver ring with the engraved gold Sanskrit letters of the OM (the sound of creation), and the message that accompanied the ring was: "Whatever Raja will do, will turn out right." Swami had also materialized a portrait of Himself containing special properties and blessings, and through the years wrote letters of encouragement to Raja.

The second lawsuit, like the first, was settled out of court. The third was withdrawn because Raja had finally decided that dharma required the full disclosure of the true motives underlying Krishnamurti's legal actions against him. When it became clear that their disclosure was imminent, the lawsuit against Raja was immediately dismissed.

Raja faced the inevitable by becoming the plaintiff in a final lawsuit, ready to fight for truth, and finally expose all the facts he had been concealing. Concealed not out of fear, as some believed, because they were all in his favor, but out of love and protection for the reputation of the man who turned against him. Raja is a man unable to bear even the slightest ill will towards those who would crucify him. Just before the suit could come to trial in 1986, Krishnamurti died; consequently, the truth will remain hidden for many years to come.

Secretly and unknown to the public, Krishnamurti asked to meet Swami and have His darshan while both were in Madras. Swami gave details of the meeting to Mother and introduced her to a teacher in His college who was present at the meeting. I am sure the meeting, in which Krishnamurti presented a rose to Swami, had a great impact on him and perhaps marked the beginning of the return.

Towards the end of March 1988, my mother left for India. Swami had told her on her previous trip, only four months before, exactly when to return. Even though Swami had asked her not to say a word about His plans to go to the mountains at Kodaikanal, she had to confide in me, as I needed to know where to reach her in an emergency since my father was not in good health.

She intuitively felt Raja was not well enough to leave in my care, as it is the wife's dharma (duty) to care for her husband. She left very reluctantly, only partially tempted by Swami's promise of their spending time together as in the "old days," as she always had a strong sense of dharma. But with the reasoning that Swami's words must be obeyed no matter what, and with my promise to notify her immediately of any change in Raja's condition (so she could have recourse to Swami's advice), she was persuaded to go.

As soon as she left, my father's health deteriorated and he stopped eating. For awhile his only nourishment was a cup of goat's milk a day, and soon he refused even that. He started to decline rapidly and before long became so weak he was unable to leave his bed.

Shortly before he lost his voice altogether, he made me promise that I would not write Mother and let her know how ill he really was. Calmly and with certainty, he told me that he knew it was his time to go, and that probably Swami had arranged that my mother be away because she would not be able to bear watching him die.

Raja had always told us that he would not want medical treatment under such conditions. He did not want to be sent to the hospital or have his life prolonged. He believed nature should be allowed to take its course, and without heroic measures on the part of the medical profession. Such restrictions are not simple and painless to bear when a loved one is involved. We, in the West, have not at all been brought up with an attitude of passive acceptance and resignation to the flow of life. We want our way, and usually struggle hard against the current to achieve it, as we firmly believe we are the "doers."

While Raja was very peaceful and accepted death calmly, I was totally distraught and desperate. Not trusting fully in my instinct that he was actually dying, I persuaded Raja for my sake, to let me call a doctor just for a diagnosis. The doctor concluded, after examination, that Raja had very advanced pneumonia. He confirmed my fear that it was very probable that Raja would go any day. He said Raja should be hospitalized immediately, yet was understanding enough to respect his wishes, to let Raja die in his own bed.

Now that I had confirmation of Raja's critical condition, I was thrown into a terrible state of confusion over my loyalty. I had promised Mother to let her know and promised my father not to. I also knew that Swami was aware of the situation, and in this case, directly planned it exactly so. But what to do? Should I let go and do nothing? To what extent are we the doers? Would I muddle things by my actions, or were even my actions predetermined?

I certainly prayed but received no clear answers as I could not be quiet long enough to receive or hear anything above my wailing. Fortunately, Robert resolved my quandary by taking action himself. He told a devotee who was leaving for India to give Mother the news of Raja's condition as soon as he arrived, thus freeing me of both my promises.

One morning (I would go two or three times a day to check on Raja), as I was walking in my father's garden with our dogs, the meaning of my mother's dream flashed clearly in my mind. Some time back, my mother had dreamt she asked Swami about Raja. Swami replied that He would call Raja indirectly after Shivaratri, and mentioned the number "three." She could not understand at the time what that meant, but suddenly I knew without a doubt, it meant the third of April. Swami had also told my mother once in Bombay, "When Raja sees Me, he will see the light." Raja had never seen Swami physically, so April 3, 1988 was Raja's appointment with the real aspect of Swami.

The resurrection of Christ (Easter Sunday) also fell on April third that year. It would be a most auspicious time for Raja, as he always had a deep love and link with Christ, after a most inspiring vision of Jesus in his youth. So, early in the morning on Easter, I left for my father's house, all the while praying for the strength to bear the pain of the loss of one of the dearest and most beloved persons in my life.

I walked slowly, choked by emotion, into Raja's room and was stupefied to behold the most beautiful and extraordinary miracle I have ever seen. My dear father, who until then had been in a comatose state and barely breathing, was now sitting up in bed as though nothing at all had happened! He had even regained the use of his voice (though a bit raspy) and was asking for food!

I knew this was Swami's doing. Even so, being always slightly skeptical of my intuition, it reaffirmed my confidence when I received proof that very day. Mother telephoned from Bangalore, and said Swami had spoken to her at great length about Raja earlier that day. Swami said He came to Ojai and brought Raja back to life. He was, indeed, supposed to have died on April 3, 1988.

This turned out to be my mother's shortest trip to India, but perhaps also the one in which she received the most grace. Swami gave Mother back her husband, wrote a personal letter to Raja and materialized special prasad for Raja's health. His great love and concern for Mother were expressed throughout many lengthy talks and, I am convinced, He changed Raja's destiny in answer to my mother's prayers.

When Robert and I returned to India in July three months later, Swami gave me the opportunity to thank Him and hear with my own ears, when He asked, "How is your Father?" I answered, "Thanks to Swami's prasad, he is much better." Swami confirmed, "Yes, he lost consciousness and had no pulse, but Swami took care."

In August 1989, Swami materialized a beautiful silver box which became filled with vibhuti as He lightly tapped on it a few times. He instructed Robert and me to tell Raja to take a pinch daily in water for maintaining his health. Swami also wrote a divinely poetic letter for Raja, which He let us read and gave permission for it to be included in this book. He surprised us when He revealed that Raja had died not once, but twice, and in fact, Swami resurrected him both times!

With Love and
Blessings
Sri Sathya Sai Baba
1-1-79

OUR BELOVED SWAMI

This Sai has come in order to achieve the supreme task of uniting the entire mankind, as one family, through the bond of brotherhood; of affirming and illumining the inner reality of each being in order to reveal the divine which is the basis on which the entire cosmos rests; and of instructing all to recognize the common Divine Heritage that binds man to man, so that man can rid himself of the animal and rise into the divine which is his goal!

Sathya Sai Baba

Silently, swiftly and deeply, like thousands of rivers, Sai workers are streaming forth from the Source, soaking the dry land with Sathya, Dharma, Shanti, Prema (truth, righteousness, peace and love).

Purely inspired by Swami, without publicity or exhibition, a monumental amount of work is being accomplished throughout India by dedicated devotees.

An educational regeneration is also taking place! Swami's university, colleges and schools are transforming and reshaping the new leaders of India to guide the future generations back to the path of morality, self-sacrifice and recognition of the brotherhood of man. History will treasure the colossal contribution this Avatar has given to mankind.

For us, Swami has been our teacher, master, guide, loving spiritual mother and father, always present to give advice and guidance in matters of the world and of the spirit, which in essence are not different—one being simply the manifested aspect of the unmanifested.

Our aim has been to learn to tap into that presence and remain immersed in its beauty, peace and silence. How quickly we proceed no longer matters, as the burden of how and when has now been placed at the feet of Sai.

Purpose, joy and love have been added to our previously empty lives by our beloved Bhagavan. What more can we ask of life than to remember and contemplate His glory?

Truly, He has manifested on earth a light in which all men may bask: reflecting brightly our light...our reality, which we have only momentarily forgotten.

I will forever treasure every precious moment with my Lord, and be eternally unable to express my gratitude for His Divine Memories.

The term Bhagavan means the One who is capable of lighting the Divine effulgence, the illumination of wisdom, the Eternal Inner

Light of the Soul. Can there be anything greater than earning the love of such an Omniscient, Omnipotent Lord? There is nothing on earth or beyond it which is equal to Divine Love. To make all endeavors to earn that love is the whole purpose and meaning of human existence.

Sathya Sai Baba

GLOSSARY

Advaita - The philosophy of non-duality
Amrita - Divine nectar of the Gods that gives immortality
Arathi - The worship of God with the flame of camphor
Ashram - A religious community
Atma - The soul which is the one infinite consciousness
Avatar - A divine incarnation
Ayah - Nanny
Baba - Father
Bal Vikas - Children educated in Swami's teachings
Bangaru - Endearing term, means "gold"
Bhagavad Gita - An important Hindu scripture containing the
   teachings of Lord Krishna
Bhagavan - The Lord, also used as a title of celebrated saints.
Bhajans - Devotional songs
Bhakti - Devotion
Brahma - The Creator in the Hindu Trinity
Brahmin - The highest of the four Hindu castes
Chitravati - A river in Puttaparthi
Darshan - Sight of a holy man
Dassara - A Hindu festival
Dharma - Duty, right action, righteousness
Dhoti - Long cloth worn as covering by men
Ganesha - A Hindu god with an elephant head who is son of
   Lord Shiva
Ganges - A Holy river in India

Gokulam - Dairy
Gopis - Cowherd girls devoted to Lord Krishna
Gulikakala - Auspicious time
Guru - A spiritual teacher
Hanuman - A devotee of Lord Rama who is part monkey part man
Japamala - Prayer beads
Jnana - The highest wisdom
Jyothi - Light
Kali Yuga - The present age, known as the age of iron or darkness
Krishna - Hindu god and Avatar
Kumkum - Vermillion powder applied to forehead
Ladu - An Indian sweet
Lila - Divine play or sport of the Lord
Lingam - An ellipsoid shaped stone worshiped as the symbol of
    creation
Mandir - Temple
Mantra - Sacred words or formula
Nirvikalpa samadhi - The highest stage of meditation
Om - The sound of creation
Om Namah Shivaya - A mantra used by devotees of Lord Shiva
Padnamaskar - Touching the feet in reverence
Panchaloha - Object made of five different metals
Poornachandra Auditorium - A large hall in Prasanthi Nilayam
Prasad - Blessed food
Prasanthi Nilayam - The abode of highest peace. The name of
    Sai Baba's ashram, located one mile from the Village of
    Puttaparthi
Prema - Love
Prema Sai - Sai Baba's future incarnation
Puja - Ritual worship
Pundit - A Hindu priest
Puttaparthi - A village in South India and location of Sai Baba's birth
Radha - Consort of Krishna and cowherd girl
Rahukala - Inauspicious time
Rama - Hindu god and Avatar of the classic *Ramayana*
Ramayana - A famous Hindu epic about the life of the Rama Avatar

Ravana - Ten-headed demon in the Indian classic _Ramayana_

Rudraksha - Type of bead used for prayer beads

Rupee - Unit of Indian currency

Sadguru - A true teacher

Sadhana - Spiritual practice

Sai - The supreme mother of all. Sai Baba means He who is both mother and father

Sai Baba of Shirdi - Sai Baba's previous incarnation which ended in 1918

Sai Gayatri - A mantra

Sai Gita or Gita - Sai Baba's pet elephant

Sai Ram - Mantra, also used as expression of greeting among Sai Baba's devotees

Sanathana Sarathi - The eternal, timeless charioteer. Name of monthly magazine published and distributed by Sai Baba's ashram

Sanyasi - One who has renounced everything and is fully immersed in God and in the discipline to attain Him

Sathya - Sai Baba's first name, also means truth

Satsang - Good company

Satwic - Pure, calm, unagitated

Shakti - Divine energy

Shankaracharya - An Indian saint

Shanti - Peace

Shiva - The transformer or destroyer of the Hindu Trinity

Shiva Gayatri - Mantra used by devotees of Lord Shiva

Shivaratri - Festival, literally "night of Shiva"

Sikh - Followers of Guru Nanak

Sita - Consort of Lord Rama

Sri - The word often used as an honorific prefix to the name of deities and eminent persons

Srimad Bhagavata - A well-known scripture dealing mainly with the life of Lord Krishna

Sundaram - Swami's residence in Madras, also means beauty

Swami - The way Sai Baba is addressed, also means a renunciant, teacher, monk

T'ai Chi - An exercise from the Taoist teachings

Telugu - Sai Baba's native language

Tiffin - Snack
Upadesh - Teachings
Vibhuti - Sacred and curative ash materialized by Sai Baba
Yamaganda - Accident time, Yama is the God of death
Yogi - A god centered man who lives a simple life of renunciation